Beyond
MY YESTERDAYS
A Woman's Journey
from Darkness to Light

JEANNIE KENELEY

New York

Beyond My Yesterdays

By Jeannie Keneley
© 2008 All rights reserved.

ISBN: 978-1-60037-407-4 (Paperback)
ISBN: 978-1-60037-408-1 (Hardcover)

Published by:

MORGAN · JAMES
THE ENTREPRENEURIAL PUBLISHER
www.morganjamespublishing.com

Morgan James Publishing, LLC
1225 Franklin Ave. Suite 325
Garden City, NY 11530-1693
800.485.4943
www.MorganJamesPublishing.com

Cover & Interior Designs by:

Megan Johnson
Johnson2Design
www.Johnson2Design.com
megan@Johnson2Design.com

Habitat
for Humanity®
Peninsula
Building Partner

ACKNOWLEDGEMENTS

*A*bove all, I want to thank the God for loving me ~ for taking all the mistakes of my past and making something beautiful out of them. He has truly turned my mourning into dancing, and I owe Him all that I am and will ever be.

When searching for an editor for this book, I only had one person that I wanted for that task. It was the man I had watched for years writing and editing copy for his clients in the advertising business. He had taught me a love for the language and passed on to me a passion for expressing myself through the written word. So to you Daddy, I am grateful not only for your attention to detail on editing this project, but more importantly for your enthusiasm and suggestions in helping me express my heart.

I am so grateful to David Hancock and the wonderful staff at Morgan James Publishing for their guidance and creative expression in designing and making this book a reality. I deeply appreciate your support and belief in bringing my story to print.

To every one of you that played a role in bringing my story to life, I say "Thank You"!

*T*his book is lovingly dedicated to my wonderful family that walked every step of this journey with me.

To My Parents –

Whose loving support and belief in me never wavered...

To My Brother and his Wife –

Who kept encouraging me regardless of how many times
I fell and had to get back up again...

To My Sister –

Who held me together when I was in a million pieces...

To My Children –

Who gave me reason to go on, whose love never faltered,
and whose lives make me so incredibly proud...

To My Grandchildren –

Whose innocent faces remind me that with each new generation
is born a new beginning...

And finally

to

"Chuck from Laguna Niguel"

The man whose love, commitment and strength have
forever transformed my life...

I love you all very, very much!

TABLE OF CONTENTS

INTRODUCTION

To put one's story onto the pages of a manuscript can be a frightening task, especially if it is not a very pretty story. One cannot change the events of their past, and even if they wanted to, it is those very events and life changing opportunities that cause us to grow and become more than we were yesterday. As we grow in our journey, we can make the decision to hide who we were in our past from all who would potentially judge us for our misguided decisions, staying safe within the cocoon of our comfortable worlds, or we can choose to follow the calling within us, to become transparent and vulnerable by stepping out in faith trusting that the path we have walked *might* have been for more than ourselves.

I am pierced to the core by the amount of abuse that we humans inflict on each other in this world, and empathize even more with every heart that endures living daily at the hands of an abuser. Words and actions can be swords that pierce the heart more deeply than any physical weapon or a fist ever could. Spouses and children are left reeling daily from being left to fend for themselves by the ones who swore to protect and provide for them. Divorce is rampant in our country where some statistics say that well over 50% of marriages end in divorce. If you are holding this book, it may be because you need to know that someone has walked this path before you, and that there is help and hope if you know where to look. Perhaps you have a loved one who is enduring the pain of watching their dreams come to an end, and you will pass this on to them.

Jesus told us that the most important of all the commandments is that we love God with all our hearts, with all our souls, and with all our minds, and that we love others as we love ourselves. As you join me on this journey, it is my prayer that you will know that I don't share the details of my life for any other reason than to encourage the heart that needs to feel loved at this very moment. The players in this story are not important. The redemption of a soul looking and longing for peace is the reason I write, trusting in a God of new beginnings, that He will take this story wherever it needs to be heard, and encourage whomever He knows it will touch. My prayer is that the Holy Spirit will settle down over your soul like a warm blanket and wrap you in His understanding, love, and grace. May the words of my story, be an expression of His heart to you.

Beyond My Yesterdays

Chapter ONE

Beyond My Yesterdays

This is a tale of two women separated by two thousand years of history, but intrinsically woven together by one shared experience.

She was a fairly attractive woman, although the years had not been particularly kind to her. Years of emotional turmoil and exposure to the desert sun had etched their marks in her once supple skin. It was a hard life, but like so many other women, she managed to make the best of it. After all, she really didn't have a choice, did she? She was a woman, but worse yet, a Samaritan woman. She really didn't hold any value to anyone, and she did what she had to do to survive.

It had been a long, tiring day as Jesus and His band of twelve made their way across the region of Samaria. With the enormous success of Jesus' ministry in the southern countryside of Judea, the religious leaders of the Jewish faith were becoming more and more uncomfortable with this self-proclaimed Messiah that healed the sick, brought sight to the blind, and claimed to forgive people's sins. These men, the holy and political elite known as the Pharisees new better than anyone the Law of Moses, handed down from their ancestors. They knew only the mighty God of Israel could forgive sins, and the protocol for such atonement demanded the strict rituals of the temple, not the casual words of a street corner-preacher! This new young rabbi's "take it to the streets" simple message of love and healing was revolutionary and seemed to them to shake its fist in the face of all they knew to be holy. Like it or not, Jesus was becoming more and more popular with the locals and the religious leaders were keeping a close watch on this man and his followers.

John the Baptist, had been heralding the coming of the Messiah to the Jewish people. People were buying into his message by the thousands. It was he that baptized Jesus as a voice from heaven had announced to the crowds that Jesus was the One that John had been telling them would come. The Jewish people were desperate for the Messiah that they believed would overthrow the government and free them from the Roman tyranny they were living under. John and Jesus' disciples were baptizing people all over the Judean countryside. With His miracles of love, forgiveness, and healing, Jesus was quickly attaining celebrity status, and the crowds were growing by the day. The Pharisees needed to do something before these growing crowds built enough momentum to threaten the status-quo. The Pharisees were astute politicians and knew better than to dare to blatantly discount this enormously popular man who claimed to be the Son of God and risk a political backlash from the people. No, something a bit more devious would be in order. Perhaps if they planted a seed of doubt in the minds of the people as to the credibility of these "holy" men, they could simply stand back and watch the fall-out! Why not post the score of baptisms that John and Jesus' disciples had performed and turn them into rivals in the eyes of the people? After all, there's nothing wrong with a little healthy competition, and everyone knows that a house divided against itself sooner or later is going to fall.

Feeling the Pharisees' hostile interest in Him and his disciples, Jesus decided to reposition the focus of His ministry further north to the area of Galilee. Perhaps a little distance from the Pharisees would enable Him along with his disciples to further their mission while providing the local religious aristocracy with a little time to cool down. The disciples were somewhat bewildered by their master's decision to take this route through Samaria. It was the quickest way, but after all, it was *Samaria*. It might have taken a bit longer, but if they could have just

Beyond My Yesterdays

headed east and crossed the Jordan, they could have skirted around Samaria altogether.

Every *good* Jew knew that Jews were to have no dealings with Samaritans. The Samaritans were considered a mongrel breed, the "dogs" of society, resulting from ancestral intermarriages between Hebrews from the northern kingdom of Israel, and the Assyrians settlers in Israel following the captivity of the northern kingdom centuries earlier. Over time, other pagans had infiltrated the land and mingled with them. These people were the outcasts of society. Samaritans had their own religion; a culturally inspired sort of mix between "Jehovah" worship and heathenism. For hundreds of years, the Jews and the Samaritans had been bitter enemies. The Jews saw the Samaritans as idolaters and hypocrites and considered even laying eyes on a Samaritan to be offensive.

Jesus knew that. They would travel through Samaria.

As the sun was high in the midday sky, Jesus and his disciples came to the historical landmark known as Jacob's Well just outside the town of Sychar. They had been traveling since early morning and they were spent. The dust of the road, mixed with the sweat of their journey, hung on them like a paste. They were dirty, hungry and tired. Jesus had been talking with his men all morning and teaching them as they walked along, and would appreciate a little time alone without the constant barrage of questions and answers. Besides, He had an appointment to keep. Sending the men into town to secure some food for lunch would give him that time alone that He needed.

As she made her way to Jacob's Well that day, she passed the men conducting business at the city gate. The freedom in their voices as they bought and sold, discussed current events, and laughed over lunch at the outdoor café in the distance, made her wonder what it must feel like to have been born male, with all the rights they possessed. It was common knowledge that many a Jewish man would start the day with a prayer to God expressing thanks that he was neither a gentile, a slave, nor a woman!

The awareness of the rising temperature broke her train of thought. The sun was getting high and unbearably hot. She'd better draw some water and get it home quickly. Her man was going to be hungry soon and he could be so mean when he was hungry.

Keeping her head bowed from the stranger sitting at the well, she went about the business of filling her water jar.

"Would you give me a drink of water?" Jesus asked. Her head rose in astonishment that this man would speak to a woman. For just a split second, she made eye contact with Him. She could see and hear in his accent that He was a Jew. Did she dare speak? After all, a Hebrew man did not talk to women in the street, not even with his mother, sister, daughter, or wife! But there was something so gentle about this Jew. In that brief second that her eyes met His, she intuitively had felt such a sense of safety come over her.

"How come you, a Jew, are asking me, a Samaritan woman, for a drink?" she asked. Years of experience had taught her to be extremely leery of the intentions of men.

"If you new the generosity of God and who I am, you would be asking *me* for a drink, and I would give you fresh, living water".

Who was this man and what was he talking about? Living water? Really!

"Sir, you don't even have a bucket to draw with, and this well is deep. So how are you going to get this "living water"? Are you a better man than our ancestor Jacob, who dug this well and drank from it, he and his sons and livestock, and passed it down to us?"

Beyond My Yesterdays

Jesus answered, "Everyone who drinks this water will get thirsty again and again. Anyone who drinks the water I give will never thirst... not ever. The water I give will be an artesian spring within, gushing fountains of endless life."

She figured she might as well humor the man. It sounded to her as though he was talking nonsense, but she best answer when spoken to. Politely, she proceeded to exchange conversation.

"Sir, give me this water so I won't ever get thirsty, won't ever have to come back to this well again!" Honestly, she thought she had heard every line a man could come up with, but this "living water" one was a new one! Oh well, he might be a bit strange, but he seemed pretty harmless. She'd better get that bucket filled and get home.

Jesus knew she would need some convincing.

"Go call your husband and then come back" He said.

Ouch! That was hitting below the belt. His suggestion pierced her soul like an arrow hitting the center of a bulls-eye.

"I have no husband," she shot back.

"That's nicely put; "I have no husband". You've had five husbands, and the man you're living with now isn't even your husband. You spoke the truth there, sure enough".

How did He know that? She had never seen Him around before. He was just passing through. He couldn't possibly know her reputation...He didn't even know her name! Something about this stranger was making her feel very uncomfortable. Her business was certainly none of his and she quickly changed the subject.

"Oh, so you're a prophet! Well, tell me this: Our ancestors worshiped God at this mountain, but you Jews insist that Jerusalem is the only place for worship, right?"

"Believe me, woman, the time is coming when you Samaritans will worship the Father neither here at this mountain nor there in Jerusalem. You worship guessing in the dark; we Jews worship in the clear light of day. God's way of salvation is made available through the Jews. But the time is coming...it has, in fact, come...when what you're called will not matter and where you go to worship will not matter. It's who you are and the way you live that count before God. Your worship must engage your spirit in the pursuit of truth. That's the kind of people the Father is out looking for: those who are simply and honestly *themselves* before Him in their worship. God is sheer being itself...Spirit. Those who worship Him must do it out of their very being, their spirits, their true selves, in adoration".

The God that this man spoke of was very different from the one she knew of. This God seemed so loving, so tolerant, even inclusive of differing cultures. She didn't miss the irony of His words. This man that knew her past was encouraging her to worship, to come before God, simply and honestly as *herself*. She had spent the better part of her life living in denial of who she was and had become. Simply and honestly herself? She didn't even know who that was anymore. That girl had died years ago.

Her skepticism was obvious from the expression on her well tanned face. "I don't know about that. I do know that the Messiah is coming. When he arrives, we'll get the whole story."

"I am He," Jesus said as his eyes met hers. "You don't have to wait any longer or look any further".

He knew that in spite of all the differing tales she had been raised with of who God was, she had never come to peace with knowing the answer. He also knew that she had never stopped longing in her soul to find that peace. Her very words had shown that she still held out hope that God would send a Messiah that would answer her questions

Beyond My Yesterdays

once and for all. Jesus, in His infinite wisdom, looked beyond her sin and saw her hunger for truth. He saw in her the little girl that once had dared to believe in the goodness of God, long before life had stolen her dreams away.

A wave of peace washed over her like she had never known. Could this man really be who he said he was? How had he known intricate details about her past that even some of the townspeople weren't aware of? It seemed as though this man was looking through her eyes right into her soul.

The voices of the disciples broke the silence as they rounded the bend with their provisions for lunch. Stopping dead in their tracks, they were shocked to see Jesus talking as openly with this Samaritan woman on the street as He would have with one of them. What was He doing? Didn't He know what kind of a woman she was? Of course He did, and they knew it. No one dared put a voice to what they were thinking, but the looks on their faces gave them away.

It was a split second that seemed like an eternity. From the gentle, forgiving, eyes of this man that claimed to be the Messiah, her attention darted to the intrusion of the disciples. Their looks of disapproval drew her quickly back to the reality of her shame. This was so familiar. Fear and a bit of panic began to set in. She'd better go. How she longed to stay and talk with this stranger some more, but the safety of their conversation had disappeared with the return of the disciples. Her heart leapt with anticipation. Could this really be the Messiah? Could her years of questions finally be over? She wanted to ask a hundred questions, but the reality of the situation she found herself in was undeniable. She feared this was no longer a safe place to be. In a state of excitement and confusion, forgetting her water pot, she ran back to town.

She could not shake off the experience of being face to face with this man that called himself the Messiah. He was so gentle, so accepting, so unlike any man she had ever met before. For the first time in years, she felt an undeniable hope welling up within her. Something in her had changed and she needed to tell someone about it. She ran back to the village telling everyone "He knew all about the things I did. He knows me inside and out!"

It was the fall of 2001. As I awoke in the guest bedroom of my parent's house, the reality of the events of the previous day fast-forwarded me into reality at lightning speed. How did this happen? How could I have made yet another choice in a marriage partner that left me scrambling with the questions of how I would survive? The man I had married just three years earlier had turned out to be someone other than who he represented himself to be. I was conned, and fell for it hook line and sinker. Over the past three years, I had given him every dollar I had spent my life working for, and he happily wasted it. I supported his business, and paid his child support from my personal accounts, all in the name of keeping my new marriage. When my money ran out, he insisted that I cash in my retirement accounts for him. That was the day that I finally said "No" to him. His anger over his loss of control festered, and he finally took it out on me. His attack on me was one of the most frightening experiences of my life. I hadn't known until that moment how weak and helpless a woman could feel, fighting against the physical strength of an angry man. I managed to get away and call 911. He was taken to jail and booked on domestic battery charges, and I was shaken to the core. I could not go back to this man.

Beyond My Yesterdays

The human psyche is amazing. When you can't take anymore, it seems to shift into an "auto-pilot" mode. You drag yourself from place to place, manage to eat a little of what's put in front of you, but mostly prefer to stay in a prolonged state of unconsciousness. Sleep was my therapy. I just wanted to escape the pain of the soap-opera that had become my life.

I remember feeling an amazing empathy induced connection to Humpty-Dumpty. I felt like all the king's horses and all the king's men could never put me back together again. My heart was shattered in a million pieces, and there I lay knowing that yet another divorce was in my future, not to mention the court dealings regarding the battery charges.

I had married the first time at the age of seventeen. He had decided that after thirteen years of marriage and two children, that he would rather spend the rest of his life with my best friend. I let him.

The second time I married, I married a man with a wonderful heart, but carefully hidden addictions that slowly eroded our marriage to the point of no return.

Now this, the impending dissolution of my third marriage. As I lay on that bed searching for the answer to every conceivable version of the question "why?", I reached for my Bible and it fell open to John 4. It was the story of the woman at the well. This was a story that I had heard many times in my life, and always sort of dismissed it as a story about a social and emotional loss of a woman that probably deserved whatever she got. After all, who in their right mind could mess up that many marriages?

It was at that moment that it suddenly dawned on me...

I *was* the woman at the well.

Beyond My Yesterdays

Chapter TWO

Beyond My Yesterdays

*a*s she hurried out of bed to prepare for the day before her man awoke, she could not have possibly known that this would be the day that would change the rest of her life.

She had been through five marriages and all the emotional turmoil that they birthed. The Bible doesn't tell us whether she had been through five divorces, or buried some of her husbands along the way, but it was clear about one thing. She was living in shame now with a man that wasn't her husband. I couldn't help but wonder about her past, her own personal story...had she been a happy child? Had she been loved? Had she been like me?

I arrived in this world on a crisp October day, born the second of three children. My childhood was like most children of the 1960's. Televisions were rare, and if your family had one, watching it was something to be considered a "treat". We actually ate dinner together each night while discussing the events of our days, or the current situation of the world at large. Daddy would put us through impromptu spelling drills as we ate, correcting our grammar as we conversed. As my little brother and I would begin paying more attention to his latest addition to his repertoire of jokes than our dinner, Mom would remind us that we were at the table to eat, not to be cutting up. More evenings than not, I remember my meal-time antics being brought to a screeching halt by my father reminding me that if I didn't straighten up, he would take me outside and let me pick the switch from the tree that he would use on my fanny if things didn't change immediately! To this day, I don't know what kind of tree that was! To me, it was the dreaded "switch tree"!

The father of my childhood was a handsome wavy-haired advertising executive. He was articulate, creative and intelligent. My earliest memories are of running to the front door every night when Daddy came home to greet him. All three of us kids would run yelling "Daddy...Daddy" in a race to see who could get to him first! In my eyes there was never a more handsome hero than Daddy, and he instilled in me a paradigm of what a loving husband and father was. In spite of whatever worldly accomplishments he may have enjoyed, I will forever remember Daddy for reasons that have less to do with how he made a living, and more to do with how he lived his life. Daddy is a man that is so in tune to the spiritual realm that he instinctively connects to your soul. He reads people as easily as he reads books. Because he loves more deeply and sensitively than many men, his model of Godly love is forever ingrained into every cell of my being. Although memories of Mother's Day would typically be about one's mother, as a child, it stands out in my mind as a tribute to my father's spirit. On Saturday before Mother's Day each year, Daddy would come home from the florist with 3 corsages and two boutonnieres, and our family would all attend church on Sunday morning decked out in flowers in honor of our mother!

My mother was a gracious, raven haired beauty that carried herself with a "Jackie-O" sort of regality. Mom was always the envy of the ladies circle at church, as no one could entertain guests like Mom could!

Beyond My Yesterdays

To this day, if you need anything for entertaining (sterling silver olive forks, sugar cube tongs?) just call Mom, she'll have it! I remember helping her clean windows and polish the silver set before the church missionary chapter came over for their monthly meeting. Mom did everything with style, and instilled an appreciation of design and detail in me. She was smart, and in a corporate world where women were held back solely because of their gender, Mom was the highest paid woman in a company of two thousand employees.

My father always taught me that I could be anything I chose to be, accomplish whatever I set my mind to, and that I should never let anyone hold me back simply because I was a girl. Mom backed that sentiment up with her example. I was blessed.

We had a very loving, but a very "churchy" home. Both of my parents were preacher's kids. Both of their father's had been hell-raisers as young men, and when the Lord got hold of their lives, the pendulum swung to the opposite extreme for both of them, and both went into the ministry. Because my parents were committed to raising their children in a Christian home and providing us with a Christian education, I was raised in very much the same manner that they had been. As a child, my parents were both Sunday School teachers, Mom held the titles of Church Treasurer and Choir Director. Daddy was the Sunday School Superintendent. We were at church every time the doors were opened, usually because Daddy had the keys!

Although that environment provided a safe cocoon for me as a child, I've always been a free spirit that was born to fly, and the confines of the church felt very stifling to me. I can remember at a very early age that the authority of the "church" and the legislated list of "don'ts" made very little logical sense to me. I was not allowed to attend movies, dances, or pierce my ears. To this day, I believe I may be the only woman in America that still hasn't seen the old Disney classics like Cinderella, Bambi, and Sleeping Beauty! I also wasn't supposed to wear jewelry or make-up, but fortunately my parents showed some leniency in those areas. I never rebelled by acting out in any destructive way (at least nothing I got caught for!), but rather challenged the traditional way of thinking by asking questions, challenging the legalism of the church that seemed to bind men rather than free them. My father loved that part of me and we would have occasional conversations about it all. My mother, on the other hand, was raised not to question authority (her father was a preacher, and preachers are next to God, you know!), and didn't quite know what to do with a child like me that questioned everything! I was that kid that always asked "Why?". I can remember more than a few times hearing a response of "Because I said so!"

I found my identity at an early age through my music. My parents were both singers and had sung on the radio for various programs back in the 1940's. They both had beautiful voices, and as it turned out, my older sister was blessed with their vocal talent. I never gave it all much thought (I was too busy climbing trees!) until one day in the third grade. I remember it like it was yesterday! I was attending a Christian school and we had a music teacher named Mrs. Brown. She came to our class, asked us to stand in a circle and sing "My Country 'Tis of Thee". As we sang, she proceeded to walk around the classroom, stopping to listen to the voice of each student as she went. As she came to me, I noticed that she lingered a bit longer than she had done with the other students. She walked on, but then took a few steps back to listen to me again. This was getting embarrassing! I thought I must have the most awful voice in the whole room for her to keep listening to me! Relief slowly set in as she moved on and finished the exercise. As she dismissed us from the circle and back to our seats, she asked me to come to the front of the room and sing for the entire class! I could have died right there on the spot. If ever I wanted the earth to open

Beyond My Yesterdays

up and swallow me, it was right then. All I can remember thinking was that if I opened my mouth, all the kids would know that my voice "shook" when I sang. I had inherited the same vibrato that made my parents and my sister known for their beautiful voices, and I was two seconds from getting laughed out of the third grade! As Mrs. Brown coached me to "project" my voice (I thought if I sang really softly, no one could hear me!) I faced the fear of the inevitable laughter head on and sang as instructed. To my shock, the class's reaction was exactly the opposite of my expectations, and from that day on, I was Jeannie the singer.

After that there was really no holding me back! I would spend count-less hours closed up in my bedroom with a "microphone" that I had fashioned from a wad of tin foil. My poor parents would have to sit through performance after performance of me singing and dancing in the living room to my Mary Poppins record! I even had a pretty mean routine of "King of the Road" where I used the vacuum for a prop that I danced around. Why the vacuum? All I can figure is that I started singing when I was supposed to be vacuuming! I just knew I was born to sing, dance, and act and it became like breathing air to me.

It was the summer of 1971. I was attending an old fashioned church "camp-meeting". The huge tabernacle was filled with thousands of worshippers, waving collapsible fans and bulletins to stave off the sum-mer heat. The piano and organ were pumping out hymn after hymn, as people stood and waved their hankies and lifted their hands as they sang praises to their Lord. It was a familiar sight to me. I was sitting through yet another sermon like the hundreds of others I had heard in my young life, but when the speaker sat down and the musicians began playing, something happened to me that I will never forget. The people began to sing...

"*Just as I am*, without one plea

But Thou my God, wouldst die for me..."

The evangelist was calling people to the altar to accept Jesus Christ as their personal Savior, and suddenly I was aware that although I had grown up in a Christian home and attended a private Christian school, I had never accepted Him personally as mine. I literally felt a hand on the middle of my back pushing me towards the altar, but ironically, no one was touching me. I knelt at that altar that day and gave my life to the Lord with all the dedication that a 13 year old girl could muster.

Adolescence is a nasty thing! It's a time where princesses turn into self-crowned queens and mothers become horrible, ugly witches. It was no different for me. As I was riding the wave of success and peer approval that my music brought me, a funny thing started happening to my wardrobe! As Grandma would have said, I just got too big for my britches! As my newfound confidence outside of home grew, my need for my mother who had been the center of my universe until then seemed less and less necessary. After all, I was making my mark at school. I kind of liked the change of going from being my parent's daughter to them being "Jeannie's parents". As this focus on roles began to change, I felt it necessary to remind my mother often of my newfound importance. Becoming more self-obsessed, I became more obnoxious. Let's suffice it to say that pushing the limits in showing disrespect to Mom was something that I became rather adept at doing! It really is a wonder that she didn't strangle me during those years!

Mom and I were eventually fortunate enough to see beyond our differences and rediscover the love that bound us as mother and daughter, but not before we both had some more growing up to do. It was during this tumultuous time between the two of us that I met a young man from out of town that swept me off my feet. I suppose I saw him as the answer to my dreams, my knight in shining armor that God sent to rescue me. After all, I just wanted to get away from Mom and what

Beyond My Yesterdays

I perceived as her need to control me. He was strong and decisive, and he had decided that he wanted me for his wife! I was 16 after all, and I was ready to make my own decisions. He could get me away from the home where I felt too protected and stifled. With him, people would see me as an adult instead of a child.

It was a 14-month courtship consisting largely of phone calls and letters, as he lived several states away and we seldom had the opportunity to see each other. Over that brief period of time, we'd see each other for 5 days here, 7 days there, always under the watchful eye of one set of parents or the other. All in all, by the time our wedding day arrived, we had spent a total of just 36 days together.

To a sixteen or seventeen year old girl, a young 19 year old man that owns his own home, his own car, and dresses like a model out of GQ can be pretty intoxicating. Every time we spent a few days together, he'd surprise me with elaborate gifts and dates to fine restaurants. In the 1970's a hundred dollars was a lot of money and this guy paid for everything with one hundred dollar bills! I WAS IN LOVE!!! This guy was as smooth as glass and in my emotional state, I was ripe for the picking.

We set our wedding date, and on August 14, 1976 at the ripe old age of 17, I jumped from the frying pan into the fire.

Over the next 27 years, I would raise two beautiful children, enjoy wonderful friendships and a loving supportive family, and know professional and financial success. However, woven through the happiness I experienced in those years, would also be the heart wrenching devastation of three marriages and divorces. I had many, many years of questions. Many times during those years, I visited with Jesus, trying to gain some understanding of what I was experiencing. There were almost 30 years where nothing made much sense to me. I saw evil people prosper, and righteous people struggle. I prayed for wisdom, but kept making bad choices. I sat in countless different psychologist's offices, looking for the answer to what was wrong with me. I sought God's guidance, but things kept going wrong. I didn't realize it at the time, but He was doing a work in me far greater than I could see then. He knew that my need went far deeper than relief from my immediate circumstances. He knew that it would take time for me to accept and deal with the lessons He had for me to learn.

What had this Samaritan woman's story been? Was she raised in a loving home or was she a child of abuse or neglect? Did she run and play with the other children? Did she spend countless hours in her own little corner of the family tent pretending to be a queen or having ladies over for tea? Did she dream of doing great things that no other woman had ever done? Did she play with a rag doll and dream of having her own family someday? Or was she just a commodity that her father used to bargain with? The one thing we do know was that women of her time were considered to be of little value save for their ability to serve.

By the time she met Jesus, I wonder how many times her heart had been broken by men that didn't even see her as a person, but rather as a tool used to satisfy their own selfish desires.

Her dreams of having a life with a loving husband were far behind her. She had been in survival mode for so long, that her hard exterior had almost convinced even *her* that she didn't really need anyone else. She could play this game of using as well as the men could. She would serve them, and they would give her a roof over her head and food to eat. At least she wouldn't be homeless; at least she wouldn't be out on the streets at night.

This day had started just as every other one had been before. She rose early to start getting breakfast on so that her man could go about his business of the day. There was laundry to do and floors to sweep. She needed some vegetables for the stew she'd make later in the afternoon. The water jug was about empty, so a trip to the well was in order. She had felt the heat of the day setting in earlier, just past sunrise. She preferred to get most of her work accomplished before noon so that she wouldn't have to be out in the sun in the worst part of the day. Her body just didn't handle the heat as well as it used to when she was younger.

This trip to the well was the same as any other, except for this Jew that asked her for a drink. Jesus met her in the comings and goings of her everyday, work-a-day world. No pressure, He was just simply and quietly *there*, waiting to have a conversation with her that would change her forever.

The heart of a woman is the most precious possession a man will ever have entrusted to him, and Jesus knew that. When she met Him at the well that day, she brought with her all the shame of her past. Too many sins to count had been perpetuated against her. Some she chose in her attempt to survive. She was a woman of virtually no worth to society. The men weren't even bothering to marry her anymore.

This man that claimed to be the Messiah her soul was longing for, knew exactly who she was, what she had done, and what her soul needed to find peace. She came to the well to quench her immediate need for water. But Jesus met her at her point of *deepest* need. He reached into the long forgotten recesses of her childhood dreams, and validated her as a person of worth. To her, He not only extended acceptance and forgiveness, but left her with the hope of a child that had never known pain. She was so amazed by the encounter, that she forgot why she came to the well! She forgot her water pot and ran to tell of her life changing experience.

Jesus looked right past her past that day, and saw the thing He most cared about...her heart... her very soul. He wasn't nearly as concerned about where she had been, as He was with where she was going. Just like the day He met me at that altar at camp-meeting, and just like all the times He's met me since, He met her *just as she was*.

Chapter
THREE

Beyond My Yesterdays

*H*ow do you explain the sting of public humiliation to someone who has never endured it? How can one tell of the gut-wrenching agony of watching your life and all your hopes and dreams fall apart as though you were a character in a bad soap opera? How can one know the feeling of being thrown away like yesterday's garbage unless you've been there?

This was all too familiar territory to this woman. Over the years, she had simply become accustomed to the sneers of the townspeople when she would pass by. The men would pretend to be incensed by her, but when no one else was around, the suggestive proposals they made to her belied their public commitment to their wives. The women in town hated her, but if the truth were told, the men in town found her intriguing. She was the town adulteress. She was attractive, and she was available. She was the forbidden fruit and she was ripe for the plucking. She was a survivor. She had known so many men, that her reputation was beyond repair.

Back in her youth, her reputation had meant so much to her. She could barely remember now the dreams of loving and being loved in return that had once filled her naïve heart. She had tried to discern right from wrong. She had been raised hearing the teachings of the religious leaders, but their hypocrisy had left her bewildered and confused. She had been taught of this mighty Jehovah of her ancestors, but now the very spiritual leaders that claimed to serve Jehovah were perpetuating sinful acts as part of their religious rituals! The man that she had pledged the rest of her life to so many years ago, had thrown her out on the street to fend for herself, and these religious leaders had supported him in his right to do so. After many years of struggling to understand this paradox of principle, she had thrown up her hands and given up on trying to make sense of it all.

Her self-esteem didn't go all at once. It was a process, much like boiling a frog by slowly turning up the heat. After years of abuse, belittling remarks and public rejection, she had become simply a shell of a human being, a dead soul walking around in a still fairly attractive body. She had tried to rebuild her life, but she had made even more bad choices in men, and her own lack of self-esteem perpetuated a seemingly endless string of dead-end relationships.

The one thing she still believed was that someday the Messiah would arrive and make sense of it all for her. What was the purpose of all of this?

I can't begin to put into words what it did to me when my first husband told me that he wanted to spend the rest of his life with my best friend. We had worked so hard to make our marriage what it should be. The only explanation he could give me for his change of heart was, "I didn't know any better than to be happy with you". Apparently he had found what would bring him happiness, and he made it clear that

Beyond My Yesterdays

it wasn't me. After 13 years of already trying to make the best of a bad choice in marrying, I don't think either of us had any more fight left in us.

To add insult to injury, when I met with our pastor to explain the situation, the pastor didn't believe me when I told him what was going on. He met with my husband who assured him that it was "all in Jeannie's head" and that he was not involved with another woman. It would take another year and a half before the woman he was involved with secured her divorce and she and my ex-husband married. It wasn't until then that our friends at church and the church leaders believed that I had indeed been telling the truth all along. I can't tell you the amount of people that came back to me at that point and asked my forgiveness for not standing by me through it all.

We had been a very focal family in the local church. My husband served on the church board, I sang in the choir, and directed the elementary kid's choir. My times with the kid's in the choir were some of the most fun times I can remember. I loved them and they returned that love tenfold to me. However, when it became public knowledge that we were divorcing, my husband and I were both asked to remove ourselves from any ministry that we were involved in. Apparently the church leaders did not want to appear as though they were siding with either of us or condoning our divorce. I had lost my husband, my best friend, my livelihood (the business we had built together stayed with my husband), my church family, and I knew I was facing life as a single mother with all the responsibility that the position carried. The betrayal was devastating and I was scared to death.

I had always believed that the church I belonged to was a place of safety from the storms of life. I loved my friends there and believed that they loved me. I trusted the church leaders to guide and counsel our family through this tough time, but learned that when people don't know what to say or don't want to be associated with your problems, they most often say nothing, or try to "fix" the problem and make it go away by slapping a band-aid of guilt on you. It was 1989 and divorce among Christians was not at all common in the small town where we lived. Since then, I have seen divorce and grief recovery programs spring up in churches nationwide, but then it was virtually unheard of. I didn't know even one person that had been through what I was experiencing at the time. At the lowest point of my life, my experience taught me that the church was the only army that would shoot it's wounded.

Just as the looks on the disciples' faces that day at the well reminded the Samaritan woman of her place in society, the cruel remarks and indifference of our church friends towards our pain reminded me with a simple glance that I was an outcast, no longer suitable for association. Suddenly I went from being one of the wives in the young mothers group to being the single mother that women didn't want their husbands being around.

For a young woman that had given the Lord her life when she was just 13 and trusted Him to guide her, none of this made any sense. I may not have been the perfect wife, but the Lord knew how hard I had tried. He knew the motives of my heart. He knew how hard it had been for 13 years. With the events of losing everything but my children, I decided that none of what I had believed in was true. How could a God that loved me let this happen? How could the God that I had served for so long hang me out to dry in the town square, open to public ridicule and leave me there? I walked away from that local congregation and didn't look back.

Shame is a cancer that eats your heart out. Whether it's shame from your own choices, or shame that you carry stemming from another's choices, it can devour your soul and destroy your hope. So we carry our secrets locked in the deepest corners of our souls, and go on, hoping that the farther we distance ourselves from the events of our past, the better we'll feel. We live in fear of being exposed for the failures that we believe we are. Maybe if we do a few more good works, it will make up for our reputations. Maybe if we give money to worthy causes, people will forget our past choices. Maybe if we just pretend long enough, we'll earn people's approval again. There's an old saying that you can fool some of the people some of the time, but you can't fool all the people all the time. When it comes down to it, the only ones we really end up fooling are ourselves.

As I began my life with my scarlet letter, I was angered by the sheer injustice of my situation. My anger and frustration led me on a journey that lasted for many years, but started by taking me through the black hole that I call the dark night of my soul.

Through the process, I learned that "depression" is just a grown-up term for saying "I'm afraid of the dark". As a child I remember trying to go to sleep at night after Mom or Daddy had turned the light out. Although in the light of day, I could see clearly that my closet housed only my clothes and various toys, at night when the lights went out, my closet was where the bears lived! If Mom or Daddy inadvertently forgot to close the closet door on their way out of my room after my goodnight prayers, I would lay there, my eyes transfixed on the dark hole of the closet, watching for the bears to come out and eat me. Once I would call for Daddy to come close my closet door, I could sleep peacefully (as long as the alligators stayed under my bed)! Children have extremely active imaginations anyway, but couple that with a dark room, and you will find that fear will emerge almost immediately.

We really aren't all that different as adults. We become paralyzed by the fears of imaginary situations, of what might happen in the future. The "dark" of the unknown scares us and plays games with our minds, often to the point of perceived hopelessness. Well-meaning friends may counsel us to "snap out of it", or do something for someone else in an attempt to get our focus off ourselves. I found through the dark night of my soul that depression is a mystery, much like the ecstasy of love. Neither can be explained, they just are. They have to be felt in order to grow through them. In both states, we feel what we feel, and no one can convince us otherwise. Where the ecstasy of love is the ultimate feeling of connection, the loneliness of depression is the ultimate feeling of disconnection.

When everything you've ever put your trust in is suddenly pulled from beneath you, leaving you spinning as to what just happened, an inconceivable fear can set in and take you to the depths of despair. How will I make it? How will my children stand any chance of having a normal life? How could "they" be so selfish as to do this to us? How could God let this happen? Why has even He betrayed and turned His back on us?

As the fear sets in, the damage to one's self esteem can lead them to do things in the name of survival that they never would have dreamed of doing before. If you have absolutely no worth to the one that abandoned you, and you feel you weren't even worth God's attention, a dangerous mindset can take hold and you may begin to believe that you are of no value to anyone...not even yourself.

It was during this time that my children literally saved my life. I so wanted the excruciating emotional pain to stop, that I began to rationalize that if I just ended my life, I would finally be at peace. Of course, this makes absolutely no sense now, but to one in the throws of the mental torture of depression, it made sense to me then. The only thing that kept me from the attempt was my children. I chose to live for them. I chose to keep going in order to provide what semblance of a normal life I could for them. They already felt like they had been abandoned once. I couldn't do that to them again. I loved them so deeply, and that love kept me going.

Beyond My Yesterdays

Instead of ending my life, I adjusted by shutting down emotionally to anyone outside of my immediate family. A hard wall of self-preservation began to build around me. My family that loved me so much could only let go and pray for me as I buried my self in my work and my kids. Although men seemed somewhat interested in me, I didn't have a lot of use for them. I learned to survive and take care of myself. I worked twelve to fourteen-hour days, six days a week and I was determined to be a financial success. I decided that I would never again put myself in a position of needing a man for anything. Life had already proven to me that they only leave you anyway. I set my jaw on being a survivor. I told my kids that we were the three musketeers and we would get through anything and everything together. During those next few years, I built and sold three more businesses, and made a fair amount of money. My retirement accounts were on track, and I had enough money to buy whatever I wanted whenever I wanted. We took nice vacations, had a nice home, and I drove a Mercedes.

Carrying this emotional "I'll show you" chip on my shoulder became a way of life for me. I kept smiling through the pain, and eventually I started opening my heart back up to the Lord, begging for some semblance of understanding and explanation of why He had allowed this gut-wrenching pain in our lives. What I didn't know at the time was that many years would pass, and I would make many more poor choices in my life before the shame would be gone. I married again, and then again, both times to men that I had no business being with. My lack of self-esteem still lingering from the severe damage and break up of my first marriage only led me into more pain and compounded shame. What's worse is that I dragged the ones I love most through it with me. My parents' hearts kept breaking for me, and my kids learned not to trust my judgment at all when it came to men. The life-lessons kept on coming, as the answers to the burning questions of my soul kept eluding me. What was wrong with me, and why couldn't I make a marriage work? I had been successful as an entrepreneur, and in every other relationship in my life. This just didn't compute!

It would be many more years before I would have my "Jacob's Well" experience sitting there on the bed in my parents' guestroom. In fact, looking back, that was the turning point where God began to make sense of my life for me, as though He were taking all the broken threads and rags of my life, and weaving them into a beautiful tapestry that finally told the story of why I had walked the path that I had. My shame had become my identity. But that morning, Jesus showed me that I no longer needed it anymore. It was time to grow beyond the labels that society had put on me. He reminded me that it was for this reason that He came, He died, and He rose again....so that I could live beyond my shame! What man had intended to hurt and harm me, He had used to mold me and sharpen me. He had kept his promise of Romans 8:28 that says, "And we know that all things work together for good to those who love God, to those who are called according to His purpose." He had a purpose for my life all along, but I couldn't see it.

Sitting there, emotionally broken, I felt the first tinge of hope as He met me there. I know how that Samaritan woman felt as all the questions of her lifetime of pain began to glimmer with a sense of purpose. We've come a long way since that morning, as there were many more lessons He had to teach me. The good news is that today, I live without the shame. He buried that somewhere at the foot of the cross, as He began to take me down a path to recovery and understanding.

Beyond My Yesterdays

Chapter
FOUR

Beyond My Yesterdays

*T*here's an old song that I can remember singing as a child in our Sunday services:

"It's just like Jesus to roll the clouds away,

It's just like Jesus to keep me day by day,

It's just like Jesus all along the way,

It's just like His great love!"

Over the journey of my life, I have found that it's "just like Jesus" to meet us in the boardroom or in the bedroom...in the mundane or in the momentous...in our sanctity and in our sin. In Romans 8:38 & 39, Paul says, "I'm absolutely convinced that nothing – nothing living or dead, angelic or demonic, today or tomorrow, high or low, think-able or unthinkable – absolutely *nothing* can get between us and God's love because of the way that Jesus our Master has embraced us."

I can now attest to that, although there have been many times over the years that I have questioned His love for me. Over the course of 27 years, I was married three different times. I have been the wife of an obsessively controlling man that needed to belittle me and ver-bally abuse me in order to elevate his own sense of self-worth. I have been a single mother, working alone to raise well-rounded children. I have been the wife of a man with a wonderful heart, but devastating addictions that he didn't choose to admit or deal with. I have been the stepmother to children, getting calls in the middle of the night to come and get the kids out of jail. I've cried with these kids, I've been there when they had to be admitted to substance abuse facilities. I've sat with their natural parents in counseling and wondered how anyone could consciously choose to parent the way they did. I've fallen prey to a con man that convincingly professed to be a dedicated Christian, only to find out a year and half into the marriage that he wasn't at all who he had said he was. By that time, he had wiped out my bank accounts and decided that physical abuse was the best way to deal with me. I have been used, emotionally and physically abused, cheated on, stolen from, and deserted.

My story isn't one of glorious redemption after a life of turning my back on God. I didn't live according to the world's ways, and then one day meet Jesus and everything was fine. I met Jesus at that altar at the age of 13. I learned at a very early age to trust the Lord to lead my life. He's been working on me for a long time! With the exception of a fairly brief time after my first divorce, I've looked to God many times a day for guidance, for clarity, and for divine discernment. It's when you look to God for guidance, and still find yourself in the midst of adversity that you begin to believe that God isn't "love" at all, but rather some sort of cosmic practical joker playing with your life. I was getting really tired of being the butt of the joke, and this had been going on for almost 30 years.

For years I could not figure out why I had one failed marriage behind me, let alone why I kept repeating the same story time after time. The leading men were different, the circumstances different, but they still had the same undertones of abuse. It reminds me of the old refrain we used to chant between verses of a song at summer camp.

"Second verse, same as the first...A little bit louder and a little bit worse!"

Beyond My Yesterdays

Through the years, the Lord used many different people to teach me the truth about love. I know that my lessons were different from some, but I have a hunch that the lessons that came together for me, were not unlike the lessons that the Samaritan woman experienced after meeting Jesus that day at the well. I had met Jesus before, but it wasn't until I started focusing daily on reading His word and allowing Him to examine my heart and motives that the pieces of the puzzle start coming together.

I had been raised attending Sunday school every week, learning about the love of God, but I must admit that it wasn't until I was deep in the despair of my first divorce that I truly had a first hand understanding of what His love really was. I had been raised in an extremely religiously legalistic environment, where I was told about the "love" of God, but never without the undertone of the "fear" of God. I remember singing a song in children's church as a child...

"Oh be careful little feet where you go,

Oh be careful little feet where you go,

For the Father up above

Is looking down on you in love,

So be careful little feet where you go!"

Forgive me for being so blunt, but what kind of screwed up theology is that? I was taught through little songs, through the theatrics of hell fire and damnation sermons, and by the attitudes of well meaning Christians that I had better be careful of every move I made, because Jesus was up there somewhere "looking down on me in love". There's an oxy-moron if I've ever heard one. Love doesn't look down on anyone.

It was during my dark night of despair that I learned a very valuable lesson about God's love.

When the hurt goes so deep that you want to die, His love goes deeper still.

My problem was that I was associating God only with the good things of life. I thought in my naïveté, that God was in all the wonderful things of life, but couldn't possibly be in the bad. My self esteem suffered greatly because every time I found myself struggling through the consequences of someone else's sin, I figured that it must have been the result of some unknown sin I had inadvertently committed along the way. Obviously God had been "looking down on me in love", didn't like what He saw, and decided to get my attention by tearing my life apart at the seams.

Over time, I came to realize that God doesn't push Himself on anyone, not even on those of us that profess to be His. That's what real love is.

People make choices that often have consequences that reach far beyond themselves. Spouses get traded for different models, and children cry themselves to sleep as they struggle to understand why Mommy or Daddy left. Single parents struggle every day to make ends meet as they keep on giving to their children from their long since depleted emotional reservoirs. Substance and sexual addictions strangle the life out of relationships every day, and yes, there really are people out there who choose to swindle, lie, and steal to get what they want in this world. You or someone you love may just be a stepping-stone on their way to where they want to go. God's heart must break with every selfish sin committed and its far-reaching effects, but He has given each of us a free will to choose what we will stand for in this life and often someone else's free will can send our lives into a downward spiral.

Beyond My Yesterdays

I had to learn that God wasn't going to be a slot-machine sort of God for me. I couldn't put in a prayer, pull the lever and have the outcome I wanted come falling out of the sky like a jackpot of nickels. There were times that I pleaded with God for justice. There were times I just wanted revenge. What I got instead was a quiet, day by day, presence of the Lord holding me as I took one day at a time, putting one foot in front of the other. When I lost everything I had ever believed in, God just let me rant and rave, as He sat quietly waiting to take me in His arms and comfort me. When I got tired of being angry, He was the soft place that I fell into to rest. That is love.

The God of my childhood was a God that couldn't look on my sin (not after I was saved anyway), let alone meet me in it. The God of my adulthood is the God that taught me that He would walk right into the sin in my life ~ be it mine or someone else's ~ and come and get me. This is the God that sent His only son right into the mess we had made of our world, just to say "I love you".

Is it just me, or do we tend to think of God as only in the good, as though he lives only in the "ups" of life? Why can't we accept that God could be in the "downs"? For me, it was when He came and met me in the depths of my despair and depression that I knew He really loved me. He wasn't there because I was good enough to merit His friendship. He was there because He loved me. No judgment. No condemnation. Just love. Without the good and the bad of life, I would not know now that *God is in the paradox.*

I have spent a lifetime reading the writings of well meaning Christian authors that perpetuate the idea that everything good in life comes from God, and that everything bad comes from Satan. Is there a Christian out there who hasn't at one time or another wondered if a negative turn of events might be God's way of expressing His disapproval of them? Is it punishment for sin? Maybe He's trying to teach me a lesson. What did I do wrong to need this lesson? Sound familiar?

King Solomon, hailed as the wisest man that had ever lived, wrote in the book of Ecclesiastes,

"To everything there is a season, a time for every purpose under heaven:

A time to be born,

And a time to die;

A time to plant,

And a time to pluck what is planted;

A time to kill,

And a time to heal;

A time to break down,

And a time to build up;

A time to weep,

And a time to laugh;

A time to mourn,

And a time to dance;

A time to cast away stones,

And a time to gather stones;

A time to embrace,

And a time to refrain from embracing;

A time to gain,

And a time to lose;

A time to keep,

And a time to throw away;

A time to tear,

Beyond My Yesterdays

And a time to sew;

A time to keep silence,

And a time to speak;

A time to love,

And a time to hate;

A time of war,

And a time of peace."

Ecclesiastes 3:1-8

Although Solomon may have been a bit of a melancholy personality, I don't think he was far from the truth when he coined the phrase "Vanity, vanity, all is vanity". I believe that what he was saying is that God is so big, so uncontainable, so powerful, that all our striving, our reasoning, our searching, and our attempts to put God in a little labeled box so that we can get our minds around who He is and what He's trying to do are completely in vain. In other words, God is sovereign; you can accept it or you can reject it, but you ain't gonna change it!

Why would a loving God that I had pledged my life to allow me to go through the years of abuse and emotional turmoil that I went through, when all I ever wanted was to love and be loved? Because He loves me and He's the only one that can see the "big picture". Why did I need those lessons? What did I do to deserve that? I was a fun loving, nice person before those hurtful years. I don't recall ever consciously setting out to hurt anyone. I was a nice girl that played by the rules, and treated others fairly well.

After all these years, I have come to a peaceful place of understanding within myself where I know this much; life isn't all about me. Life is about Him. I have discovered that my purpose in this life is to learn the lessons designed for me, to apply those lessons to my life, and to grow each day to become more like Him. Only in doing that will I accomplish what I'm ultimately here for; to be a compass for others that points the way home. Where I live, the car I drive, the job I hold, the family I have, the friends I enjoy, the traveling I've had the privilege of experiencing, the successes I've known, all the great things I hold dear in this little bubble of mine that I call "my life" are wonderful blessings straight from the Creator Himself to me. But looking back, the *greater* gifts that He sent me were the years of heartache, the broken relationships, the disappointments in my work, and the loss of "my" dreams along the way.

You see, I now understand what Paul meant when He said that "His strength is made perfect in my weakness". If I hadn't been through the fire of those years, I would not have the deep sense of self and peace that I enjoy today. It's a great feeling to know who you are and Whose you are. What a gift to realize that you really are a part of something much bigger than yourself.

How can I look at my past experiences as gifts? Because hindsight is always 20/20! You see, the people that hurt me the most deeply in my past turned out to be the greatest teachers of my life. As a direct result of their impact on my life, I was forced to wrestle with issues like forgiveness, my paradigm of Christianity, my sense of self-worth and identity, tough love, drawing boundaries, and surrender. Because of *them*, I am who I am today. I have often said that I wouldn't wish any of my heart-wrenching experiences on anyone, but I *would* wish the deeply satisfying results of those experiences on everyone.

I, like Paul, have prayed many times during my lifetime that God would remove that "thorn in my flesh". What I finally realized is that He didn't remove it because He allowed it to be there in the first place to teach me something. When I finally got the lesson, the pain was gone. God was in the paradox all along, *because He loved me!*

Beyond My Yesterdays

Chapter FIVE

Beyond My Yesterdays

FORGIVENESS 101

To err is human, to forgive divine.

– Alexander Pope

*J*esus was the only man that has ever lived or will ever live that *didn't* mess up. Our sins come in various forms. Some are what we would consider to be trivial. Others may be larger, but we choose them anyway because we somehow feel entitled to them. We rationalize that if God loves us, he'll love us no matter what we do. Some of us are so sensitive to wanting to please God that we tip-toe through life afraid of doing anything for fear that we might sin without even being aware of it! On the other extreme, there are others who will shake their fists in the face of God, just daring Him to love them and prove that He is what He says He is. Some simply come to a point of sheer frustration from trying to figure out a world where evil people prosper, and the good struggle, and consequently give up. For a myriad of reasons, we have all at one time or another known that feeling in our gut when we know that we've messed up. Many of us still live daily with the consequences of our past choices that forever changed our lives. We should have walked away from a temptation, should have kept our mouth shut, and should have resisted the need to put someone in his or her place. Would-a, could-a, should-a.

I have found over the many years of my life that God does not direct us to stay away from sin because He loves to control us like little puppets in some sadistic cosmic theatrical production. He instructs us in the "paths of righteousness" because He loves us. It is for our very protection that He leads us. It is for our very protection that He has given us His word to be a "lamp unto my feet, and a light unto my path".

In my life, I have known the feeling of being a repentant sinner. I have known the feeling of being an unrepentant sinner. It was however through the experience of being the victim of the fallout of other's misguided choices that I learned the true meaning of forgiveness.

As a young girl of 13, when I knelt at that camp meeting altar and asked for forgiveness of my sins, I must admit that I didn't really have any understanding of what Christ had done for me. I knew that He had given His life for me, to save me from my just desserts, but how bad could I have possibly been at 13? I was a good child from a Christian home, attended church 8 or 9 times a week (OK, that might be a slight exaggeration), and the only sin I could ever remember committing was having stolen a piece of bubble gum from one of my Sunday School teacher's classrooms. Somehow, the bubble gum incident seemed justified in my mind. After all, I had sat through hundreds of dull classes in that room!

It would be many years later before I would truly begin to understand the enormity of what Christ had done for me on that cross. In leading me through one of the most horrific experiences of my life, He showed me just a minute glimpse of what He felt going through the process of His trial and crucifixion.

Betrayal by someone that you love and trust is one of the most gut wrenching experiences that a person can endure, especially when you've done everything humanly possible to make that relationship a good one. But when I was faced with being betrayed by my husband, and he had betrayed me by falling in love with my best friend, it was more than I could take. Somehow, his betrayal didn't surprise me all that much. Something inside me had always known that he didn't really love me as a person, but rather loved me playing the role that he had chosen for me. He never really even knew me. After thirteen years of marriage, I asked him why he had married me in the first place. He said, "I don't know, I guess I thought you had the potential to be what I wanted in a wife".

I had grown so accustomed to living in denial, to always believing that if I just somehow could please him, that He would finally love me, and I would feel that calm, assuring feeling of security that you feel when you know that you are emotionally safe. We were young, had two beautiful children, a house on the hill, a successful business, and by all outward appearances, were the "perfect" family. Funny thing about denial, sooner or later, life has a way of making you look reality square in the face and deal with it.

The entire experience could have been much less painful if he would have just taken responsibility for his choices. If he had been able to look me in the eye, tell me that he didn't love me, and that he wanted the divorce, I could have handled it better than the way it happened. Instead, he denied that he even wanted the divorce to everyone but me. He went out of his way to paint me as a bad mother and wife in an attempt to justify what was happening. The mental torture I went through listening to him tell me of his latest "lunch" with her, their last kiss, what she meant to him was sheer anguish to me. He denied his love to me while publicly denying his love for her.

It was during this time that I had a dream that I will never forget. In my dream, my husband, my best friend and I were out in a beautiful meadow on a beautiful day. We were running and laughing and enjoying just being together as though we were children squeezing every ounce of daylight we could out of a warm summer day. The sky was blue, daisies dotted the grassy landscape, and all was right with the world. As we ran along, my friend saw a grassy hill and ran to the top to see the view. She called to my husband to come and see. He yelled back to me to come up and enjoy the view, too. I ran as fast as I could, laughing as they pointed out the horizon ahead of me, telling me how beautiful it was. I could hardly wait to reach the top of the hill to see what they were seeing. But just as I reached the pinnacle of the hill, each of them took one of my arms, turned me around backwards and threw me to the ground on my back. What I hadn't seen was a cross laying in the thick grass that they now had me pinned against.

They took turns nailing my hands into the cross, and then raised it, leaving me to hang there. As they wiped their hands, they ran hand-in-hand back down the hill, laughing as I cried out to them.

As I awoke in a sweat, I realized that my dream wasn't too far from reality. As we hadn't separated yet, I remember crying and sharing my dream with my husband. For one brief moment, we connected and he told me that he understood why I felt so betrayed. But once the light of day shone through the windows of our bedroom, life was back to business as usual.

I have thought about that dream many times over the years. Looking back, my dream screams of my feelings of being completely out of control of my life. But more than that, I believe it tells the story of my complete shock at what was happening to me. How could this happen to me when I had trusted my life to the Lord and believed that He would never leave me? I begged my husband to give her up and do what was right for our family, but he told me that he would be done with her when he wanted to be done with her, and that I would stay with him because I was his wife and I owed it to him. One minute he'd want a divorce, the next he just wanted both of us. I couldn't take it.

I understood the temptation of being attracted to someone else. I had experienced the same thing years earlier in our marriage, but when faced with the temptation to act on those feelings, I chose my marriage

Beyond My Yesterdays

and my family. We had sought help through marriage counselors, and both worked to make our relationship what it should be.

I don't know why my sub-conscious conjured up a cross to symbolize what was happening to me, but I do remember waking from that dream and having a whole new understanding for what Christ went through as He was betrayed to death. Don't get me wrong. I'm not putting my set of circumstances in the same category as what my Lord went through, but it did make me think. Imagine what He felt as someone that He loved and trusted sold him for barely enough money to buy an injured slave. This person that He had poured His love, time, and wisdom into. This person that He had invested His very life in. If anyone in your life has ever tossed you aside like a piece of worthless garbage, you will have just the tiniest glimpse of one of the emotions that He endured for us. The sheer mental torture of watching spiritual warfare being played out right in front of your eyes, and knowing that "good" is not going to win this particular battle, simply because of someone else's free will and right to choose can be unbearable. Is it any wonder that Christ sweat drops of blood when He felt the sins of people that He loved multiplied infinitely before He went to Calvary? What a gamut of emotions. All of them feeling completely hopeless. As I thought of Him hanging there crying "My God, My God, why have you forsaken me?", I felt so alone. My heart echoed His cry over and over.

It was out of my control. I truly believed that these two people had torn my life apart and that God had deserted me, and eventually my hurt turned to anger. For the most part, I channeled that anger into survival, pouring myself into my work to ensure a standard of living for my children. I had such a fear of losing my children, and I wasn't about to give my former husband any ammunition to take my children from me. Fear was the only thing that kept me going through those early years after the divorce.

When you share children, a divorce is never really over. If both sides can come to a point of true forgiveness, the shared times that you spend together can be spent as an extended family and the needless pain of harbored grudges doesn't have to taint your present or your future. Unfortunately, I know very few parents that have ever reached this state of enlightenment, and the ones that suffer the most from it are the children. I'm not sure exactly when this realization dawned on me, but I remember that when it did, I made a commitment to change my attitude towards my former husband and friend for the sake of my children. I knew that I couldn't change my outward attitudes without a major spiritual overhaul of my heart. I knew that I had to forgive them.

Talk about "easier said than done"! I have learned over the years that to err may be human, but to forgive is *impossible* without the Divine. I'm not talking about forgiving the person that took the parking space you were waiting for at the supermarket. I'm talking about forgiving the ones that have made conscious choices that have torn your life apart, hurt your children, shattered your dreams, and abused your love and trust.

I told the Lord that if He wanted me to forgive them, He'd have to change me. I knew I didn't have it in me. I thought a lot about forgiveness. I thought about how Jesus taught us to pray that God would "forgive us our trespasses, *as* we forgive those who trespass against us". Ouch.

I made the steps necessary to ask for forgiveness. I hadn't chosen their affair, or our divorce, but I had played a key role in it. I was destroyed, but I had reacted to it all as most people would. Let's say my behavior was less than stellar throughout the process, and I knew I needed to ask my ex-husband and his new wife for forgiveness for my part of the hurt that had transpired between us. I did that. I wish it had stopped there, but it didn't. He never admitted any wrongdoing on his part to me. He never asked for my forgiveness. To this day, nothing seems much different than it did before I asked for their forgiveness.

I didn't remarry for several years, so every time I would attend one of my son's baseball or basketball games, or my daughter's school concerts, I would be there alone. They would be there together. For years, they would go out of their way to treat me rudely, ignoring me when I was standing right in front of them. Fortunately, over the years, my children saw through the hate and their treatment of me. In the long run, I believe their behavior ended up saying far more to our children about them than it ever did about me.

What God had to teach me through the process, was that I didn't need to spend my time worrying about them. He wanted to show me things about myself that I needed to work on if I was going to continue to follow Him in my pursuit of my own emotional growth and health. Every time I felt the sting of their hate and rejection, I fought that much harder to live above the very human emotions that I was experiencing. One day, as I was reading my Bible, the Lord gave me the gift of letting me stumble across Genesis 19 and the story of Sodom and Gomorrah.

It's a familiar story to many. God told Lot to take his wife and daughters and to flee the cities of Sodom and Gomorrah, as God was about to destroy these cities known for their wickedness and sin. God was specific in His orders to flee and to not look back. Lot did as God commanded, but as his wife reached the summit of the hill as they were escaping God's wrath, she did exactly as God had commanded her not to, and she turned to look back at what she had left behind. In an instant she was transformed into a pillar of salt.

Suddenly, I was Lot's wife. It had been years since the truth of our marriage relationship and divorce had driven me from everything I had held dear. But I kept turning around to look at my past, letting it define who I was. I realized that I had learned to wear the sting of my past experience like a badge of honor. Look at what I had given up. Look at what I had been cheated out of. Just look at what "they" did to me. A gracious God showed me at that moment that not unlike Lot's wife, in my insistence on letting my past define my present, holding onto my hurt like a child holds tightly to her security blanket, I too had become hard and bitter. Like Lot's wife standing there as a monument to her inability to let go of her past, so was I.

God, in His own gentle way, showed me that because He loved me, I needed to forgive these people who had hurt me, not for their sakes, but for my own. He showed me I John 4:20 & 21 where it says, "If someone says, "I love God", and hates his brother, he is a *liar*; for he who does not love his brother whom he has seen, how can he love God whom he has not seen? And this commandment we have from Him; that he who loves God *must* love his brother also." It was as plain as the words I was reading directly from the word of God. No room for interpretation, no room for justification. If I was going to continue to grow in Christ, I would have to let go of my hurt and my hate.

The hurt didn't go away, in fact it continued every time I saw them. What did go away was the hold it had on me. It didn't happen all at once, but today my past is not what defines me. Rather, it's an experience that I share in hopes that someone else will benefit from the lessons I learned along the way. Today I can bless and pray for their marriage, as I know that their happiness will ultimately benefit our children and our grandchildren. As they continue to grow in their spiritual journey, they are also growing to be more like Christ. I realize that they are not the same people they once were either.

Forgiveness can be the hardest thing one will ever do, but the good news is that it is possible. If we let go of our wounds of the past that

Beyond My Yesterdays

define us, and allow God through His Holy Spirit to guide us gently into emotional health, there is a brighter day ahead. I am no longer defined by my hurts, but rather by my relationship with the One who took all the scars of my past and turned them into a treasure of experiences that will guide my future.

To err may be human, but to forgive can be the most excruciatingly freeing experience God can lead one through.

Beyond My Yesterdays

Chapter

SIX

Beyond My Yesterdays

*T*hou shalt not lie. It's best known as the 9th commandment.

Prov. 6:16 & 17 states that one of the seven things that the Lord hates, in fact finds an *abomination* is a lying tongue.

Titus 1:2 says that God Himself is *incapable* of telling a lie.

I John 5:6 states that "...the Spirit is *truth*."

Phillipians 2:5 says to "Let this mind be in you which was also in Christ Jesus..."

I Peter 1:16 says "Be holy, for I am holy".

No matter what your bent, or how you slice it and dice it, as Christians we are to live in *truth*.

As a child raised in a Christian home, I learned at a very early age that any lie told for any reason in our household would be quickly and swiftly dealt with. Not unlike Pavlov's dog, I quickly learned that certain actions would yield certain consequences, and therefore I was trained without too much difficulty to speak the truth most of the time. Although I can remember telling a white lie or two, I remember more the need my mother often had to keep me from voicing my perception of the truth at inopportune moments spent with family and friends. I was one of those kids that pretty much said everything that came to their mind, and figured that if the truth was obvious to me, I might as well enlighten all others present to my opinion.

As a child, I remember one incident in church before the Sunday evening service. I had gone home with family friends for the afternoon, and returned to church for the Sunday night service. I saw my mother across the church, speaking with a friend of hers. It came to my attention that my mother must have colored her hair that afternoon, as there was a bit of a blue hue to her normally black hair. Figuring she needed me to point this out, I called to her across the church, "Hey Mom... why is your hair blue?" With all eyes focused on Mom, I got that look that told me she hadn't appreciated me pointing her "do" out in front of the entire congregation. Raising me had to be a lot of fun. For me, learning to speak the truth was not as big of a challenge as learning to speak the truth in love, or better yet, knowing when to keep my mouth shut!

Although I never thought of myself as a liar, it was only a few short years ago that I had one of those light bulb moments, where I realized that most of the pain that I had known in my life could have been avoided, had I not been lying to myself. As I began to retrace the steps that led to the monumental decisions I had made in my life, I realized that the Holy Spirit had waved many red flags in front of me to alert me to danger, but I had brushed them away as though swatting a pesky fly. Spiritual discernment was not my forte'. I'm not sure it was even on my radar screen!

Looking back over the choices I had made in marriage partners, I had to come to the place of taking full responsibility for the choices I had made. This came through much soul searching and analyzation into why I made these choices. Why had I chosen the path that I had? Why had I had three marriages where I spent my time in the relationship catering to other's selfish desires and addictions, being neither respected nor truly loved? I can't begin to tell you how many hours and dollars were spent over 20 years of my life in therapy asking pro-

Beyond My Yesterdays

fessional psychologists to tell me what was wrong with me! I've never been much for beating around the bush. I just wanted a straightforward answer! I searched everywhere for someone to spell it out for me, in black and white, giving me the key that would unlock the door to an emotionally healthy future for myself. I had lived according to the rules. I hadn't entered into any of my marriages with a half-hearted commitment. I had entered into each of them determined to build a loving Christ centered home and marriage. Divorce was the farthest thing from my mind.

It was during the demise of my third marriage that I was sitting in the office of Fran Jones, a psychologist and a beautiful Christian woman. She would pray with me during each of our sessions together, always encouraging me in the midst of my struggle. She had also counseled my husband, and was lovingly honest and understanding with me as I worked to keep my marriage commitment. I was so tired of asking different Christian counselors to tell me what was wrong with me, only to be told "There's nothing wrong with you, Jeannie". It didn't make sense. After all, *I* was the one common denominator in all three marriages!

In my exhaustion and frustration that day, I remember asking, "Fran, what is wrong with me? I keep marrying men that don't respect or truly love me!" I am convinced that God put the words into her mouth that I so desperately needed to hear that day.

"Jeannie, what is it that *you don't respect and love about yourself* that would cause you to choose these men?" Fran asked me.

All the lies that I had been telling myself for nearly thirty years began to rain down on me. It wasn't painful. I actually found it refreshing. For the first time, my life started to make sense to me.

As my mind went back to my courtship before my first marriage, I had seen signs of my boyfriend's tendency to control others with his moods. I had felt the sting of his glare of disapproval, often leaving me to wonder what I had done. I had learned that he had dated many of the girls in town before he found me, the California girl. I had also noticed that he hated every girl that had ever broken up with him. His grudges didn't seem to go away. I sensed before we were married that we would end up divorced, but when we discussed it, he assured me that *he* would never get divorced. The night before we were married, I was joking with my grandfather during our wedding rehearsal dinner. My soon to be husband, while painfully squeezing my leg under the table, leaned over and whispered in my ear "You might as well learn right now, that wives are to be seen and not heard". The writing was on the wall; I just chose not to read it. I told myself that he would be different with me. He said he loved me. Wasn't that all we would need to make a happy life for each other and our children? He seemed so self-assured. I was so confused. My gut told me that I was making a mistake, but I chose to ignore my own intuition and to turn the reigns of my life over to this young man that spoke and acted with such confidence. Years later as I pleaded with God to tell me why this divorce happened, the thought never occurred to me that He had tried to warn me beforehand that this was not His best choice for me.

I have realized through time that there is a real difference between the *perfect* will of God for our lives, and the *permissive* will of God. You see, what would have been the perfect will of God for us can often be overshadowed by our need to have what we want when we want it. Rather than wait for His timing, or His best for us, we take matters into our own hands and ask Him to put His seal of approval on it. It's at times like these, that although He would rather give us His best, He will always honor our right to choose our own path, and then it becomes His *permissive* will. He has all the time in the world, and He knows we will learn our lessons when we're ready.

Beyond My Yesterdays

Years went on, and I kept repeating the lesson until I got it. The signs were always there, but in my desperation to be loved and accepted, I would convince myself that things would be different with this one. I repeatedly gave myself away to the lowest bidder, and always paid the ultimate price of failure for it.

Why do we kid ourselves? Most of us would never think of making the conscious choice of lying to anyone else. Why do we do it to ourselves?

A few years ago, Bruce Wilkinson wrote *The Prayer of Jabez*. In this small book that has swept the world, Dr. Wilkinson drew powerful life lessons from the prayer of this little known biblical character for experiencing God's best for our lives.

I Chronicles 4:10 reads... And Jabez called on the God of Israel saying "O that You would bless me indeed, and enlarge my territory, that Your hand would be upon me, and that You would *keep me from evil, that I may not cause pain.*"

I've thought often of how this prayer so coincides with the way that Jesus taught us to pray, "lead us not into temptation, but deliver us from evil".

As I have reflected on these two prayers, I have spent a lot of time thinking about our need for God to protect us from evil. I have learned that even Christians that are seeking God's will often fail to recognize it when it's right in front of them. In reflecting on the prayer of Jabez, the phrase that stands out in my mind is ...*that I may not cause pain.* In looking back over my life, I can't begin to count the times that I have caused others pain because of my poor choices. But the deeper truth here for me is that because I listened to the lies of my own ego, convincing myself that I possessed the intellect and the wisdom to make life changing decisions even when confronted with my

Spirit-given intuition telling me otherwise, I have caused *myself* more pain than I could ever have imagined possible.

Being a "type A" personality, I am focused, driven, and can pretty much win at whatever I decide to compete for. When I see a goal, I just aim towards it and run full speed ahead. The lesson for me in this respect has been that outside of God, and waiting for His perfect will for my life, *I am nothing*. I have proven my inability to run this race called "life" without Him over and over. Don't get me wrong; I consulted Him, sort of. It might be more accurate to say that I chose my path and then asked Him to bless it. I have consequently personally paraphrased the verse "keep me from evil, that I may not cause pain" to read "keep me from *myself*, that I may not cause pain." I have learned the hard way that waiting for God's best for me is the only way to go, despite my natural tendency to want to get from point A to point Z in the quickest amount of time possible.

In searching for God's will, we most often turn to the Bible and look for answers. After all, this is God's word, and we know we should be able to find answers there. But, guess what! Life isn't always black and white, and we won't always find the answer to our exact dilemma jumping off the page as we open our Bibles to search the scriptures.

This is why Jesus told us that He would send the Holy Spirit to guide us. In John 14:26 He tells us, "But the Helper, the Holy Spirit, whom the Father will send in My name, He will teach you all things, and bring to your remembrance all things that I said to you". He continues in John 16:13-15 "However, when He, the Spirit of truth, has come, He will guide you into all truth; for He will not speak on His own authority, but whatever He hears He will speak; and He will tell you things to come. He will glorify Me, for He will take of what is Mine and declare it to you. All things that the Father has are Mine. Therefore I said that He will take of Mine and declare it to you."

I have learned that living a victorious Christian life outside of a consistent, sold out, relationship with Jesus Christ is impossible. Learning to give up our own selfish desires and illusions of superiority is for many of us, the hardest lesson we will ever learn. The beauty of this Christianity thing is that when Jesus ascended back to the Father, He promised that God would send the Holy Spirit as a guide to help us through life.

In my life I have found that when I can't find an answer I'm looking for, the smartest thing for me to do is to lay it at the foot of the cross, leave it there and ask for the Holy Spirit to guide me into the truth for my circumstance. I have not always found my answer in the Bible. Sometimes, my answer is in the word of a friend, the pages of a book, a song I hear as I'm driving down the road, or a line from a movie that jumps out at me. You see, I believe that when we are truly surrendered to listening for the voice of the Holy Spirit, and are willing to wait for it, He'll very often send our answer through an extremely unconventional and most unpredictable way! When we know Him, we know His voice when He speaks to us. We may not want or even choose to listen to it, but if we're honest with ourselves, we *know*.

Sometimes, I simply have to be acutely aware of the intuition that God gave me in the first place to warn me against impending doom. As I look back over my life, there have been many times that my intuition told me something that I didn't heed. I would pray about it, talk to friends and family about it, worry and fret over it. All the while, following my initial intuition about the circumstance would have been the best answer for all involved. Is it really so hard to believe that God might answer my prayer before I even pray it? I believe we call that being too close to the forest to see the trees! Why do we spend so much time crying out for God when He's right in front of us? He put that intuition in us for a reason. But how do we trust our own intuition?

Romans 12:2 tells us "And do not be conformed to this world, but be transformed by the renewing of your mind, that you may prove what is that good and acceptable and perfect will of God."

I can relate to Eve, when the serpent managed to convince her that God didn't really mean what He said when He told her not to eat of the fruit of the tree. When left to our own devices, trusting in our own "wisdom", we are leaving our minds open for Satan to slither his way into the recesses of our reasoning, taking over our ability to make sound decisions. As Christians we are called to study, dissect, and question the word of God. Some would think this dangerous. I have found that the more I question, the more His word is revealed as truth to me. The more I search for truth, the more I find in Him, and it is through this very process that my mind has been transformed. Instead of being conformed to this world, caught up in the piety of our own thinking, we can search for truth and be transformed so we know what is the good and acceptable and perfect will of God.

Each of us has been given the gift of intellect and reason, and we are to use it. My Dad used to tell me to "Keep an open mind...just not so open that your brains fall out"! We should be extremely discerning in where we look for truth. Everybody seems to be selling "truth" these days, but I have learned through first hand experience that deceit is around every corner, and very often cloaked in the cover of religion. When we begin to search for truth in an attitude of humility and openness, God will reveal Himself as "the Way, the *Truth*, and the Life".

No more lies. The truth of my story? I hadn't loved and respected *myself* enough at the age of 17 to walk away from the unhealthy relationship that would become my first marriage. I *chose* not to trust my own intuition and God honored my right to make that choice. After thirteen years of feeling invisible and unworthy in that marriage and hearing my husband tell me that he didn't want to be married to me anymore, divorcing only magnified my sense of insecurity and low self esteem. I grew over time to *believe* I was unworthy of my husband's or God's love, and it took a couple more horrifically bad personal choices before the light went on and I realized that the problem in my life was rooted far deeper than my choice in marriage partners. It was time I do some real soul searching. I was done lying to myself.

Beyond My Yesterdays

Chapter SEVEN

Beyond My Yesterdays

DRAWING A LINE IN THE SAND

*I*t was the most beautiful place on earth. As far as the eye could see, the lush landscape seemed to breathe in rhythm to the fragrant melody of the song of life. Birds singing... crickets chirping... the sound of a waterfall cascading to the rocks below. The lion and the lamb, the giraffe and the ant, were there living in perfect harmony. There were trees to shade and grow vines for the monkeys to swing from. There were fish and fowl, daisies and dandelions. And He saw that it was good. In the center of it all stood the crowning glory of God's creation. Their names were Adam and Eve. Created in His image; the most beautiful specimens of humanity that would ever be seen. It was literally heaven on earth, untouched by evil, just the blissful union of God and nature. And He saw that it was *very* good.

Then in His infinite wisdom and love, God drew a line in the sand.

He placed no restrictions on them, save for one. They were not to eat the fruit of one particular tree. He had given them an abundance of food in herbs, fruits, vegetables, and dominion over the entire animal kingdom. They could eat wherever they wanted, whenever they wanted from their waking moment to the midnight buffet. However, God warned them that if they ate from the "tree of the knowledge of good and evil", they would surely die.

Yes, since the dawn of time, boundaries have protected us from others, from evil, and from ourselves.

I had some major lessons to learn about boundaries and about truly loving myself.

Sitting in church one Sunday, I heard a sermon based on Matthew 22:37-40. It's a familiar passage where Jesus was asked which of the ten commandments handed down to Moses was the most important. He said, "Love the Lord your God with all your passion and prayer and intelligence. Love others as well as you love yourself. These two commands are pegs; everything in God's Law and the Prophets hangs from them".

This well-meaning minister was going on about loving others as we love ourselves. He said that loving ourselves is a "no-brainer." His argument was that if we don't think we love ourselves, just look at the way we fuss and muss over every thing in our lives. That alone would prove that we love ourselves sufficiently. His point was that He felt that Jesus was saying that if we just turn our focus onto others as much as we focus on ourselves, everything will be fine. He stated that it was really quite "simple".

I beg to differ. As I sat there listening to him speak of how loving ourselves is a "no-brainer", I thought to myself that this man had obviously never endured years of emotional abuse. I agree with Christ that our goal in life should be love, but I also believe that one cannot give away that which one does not possess.

This world is full of people that have been used, abused, and stepped on by selfish people looking for a step up. Why is it that women in particular seem to fall prey to becoming the fallout of other peoples' quests for dominance? Perhaps it is because we are the nurturers and the emotional backbones of our families. We were created by God to be *tender*, to sense our loved ones' needs, and then minister to them. The majority of the women I've known in my lifetime have no problem at all loving and serving others, but rather have the op-

Beyond My Yesterdays

posite problem. We don't love and treat ourselves as well as we treat others! We raise our children to set boundaries for themselves in our attempt to mold them into people of character, but we often fail to set boundaries for ourselves that reflect that same commitment to love and respect ourselves. This may be especially true for those of us that have found ourselves in repeated situations of abuse.

I am not a psychologist, and cannot speak clinically as to what happens emotionally when a person is abused. I can only speak from experience. When one goes into a relationship wanting nothing more than to love and be loved, reality can cut like a knife when it hits.

For me, I went into marriage as an outspoken person that voiced her opinion and stood up for herself. I was a strong woman, and quickly learned that my strength was not going to be tolerated. When it became apparent that my opinion wasn't wanted, it cut me to the deepest part of my being. I was learning through a slow process that I wasn't valued outside of my service to my husband. Everything in our lives centered around him. I would constantly ask him what he was thinking, taking his emotional "temperature" to see if I was measuring up in his eyes. I just wanted him to be happy. I did everything in my power to please him. My Christian upbringing at that point became as much a detriment to me as an anchor. In my attempt to be Christ-like, I adopted an attitude of survival, all in the name of Christ. I was a Christian, and thought it was my job to make this marriage work!

I took that responsibility seriously. However, I made the mistake of equating my husband's will with God's will. I began giving so many pieces of myself away in the name of keeping harmony in my marriage, that it wasn't long before I didn't even know who I was anymore. Thinking that this was pleasing to God, I sank into a life of defeat and martyrdom. When you no longer have any sense of who you were created to be, you come to the point where it's easier not to care anymore than to think about it and hurt. You stuff the pain deeper and deeper, hoping that it will go away. I remember praying almost daily that one of us would die. I didn't care if it was me or my husband, I just wanted God to make the pain stop.

Finally, our eventual divorce broke the chain of the daily experience of living in that emotional bondage. I felt like a bird that had been let out of a cage. However, I had no idea at the time that it would take *years* of healing from those 13 years of marriage before I would come back to the place of being able to love myself and love my life again. Those emotional tapes in my head played on, over and over. It took everything in me to fight my way back to a sense of well being and learn to unlearn what I had grown to believe about myself.

Christ called us to love others *as ourselves*, not instead of ourselves. We are not called to be doormats. We are called to love, and sometimes that love has to be tough. It might be a bit tough on others. It might be tough on us. Part of this process for me was learning to reclaim the person that God created me to be. Over the years I learned the importance of drawing boundaries for myself. I started with baby steps. I got stronger through the years. Eventually, I got to the point that nothing and no one crossed the boundaries that God had taught me to draw in my life. It was a process of learning about love...*true* love. God's love for me, my love for Him, my love for myself, and my love for others.

I had learned that if I was going to love others *as myself*, I needed first to love myself enough to draw a line in the sand when it needed to be drawn.

My biggest failure in drawing boundaries had manifested itself in my inability to say no to men. Before I left home at 17, I had never experienced the need to do that before. My father and my brother were the only men in my life, and our relationships were grounded in love and respect for each other. That was all I knew. I wasn't one of those people that can't relate to God as "Father" because their earthly father had been absent in one way or another. I had a father that I adored, and he had never been unfair with me in any way, shape or form. That was how I saw God, and I married *assuming* all men loved their wives and families the way Daddy loved us. My venture into the real world was devastatingly eye opening for me. I was more worried about being accepted in other's eyes than being true to my own convictions. After my first divorce, I would date men simply because I didn't want to hurt their feelings by saying "No, thank you" to their invitations to date. I had such a deep need to be accepted that I didn't see myself as worthy enough to turn down their invitations! I wasn't overly promiscuous, I just dated men that I had no common values with simply because I so wanted to feel accepted by someone. I lived a Christian life, but only to the point where God's laws started interfering with my need to feel loved and accepted.

As I look back over the years and marriages of my life, I have realized one thing for sure. The reason I kept repeating the same lesson, was because I *was* loving those men as I loved myself! From my own pit of emotional need, I subconsciously sought out men that I thought I could "help". Sometimes I think when we can't control our own circumstances, we look for someone worse off than ourselves, and subconsciously transfer our own feelings of unworthiness to them. I think that in hooking up with men that were emotionally worse off than I, it gave me some strange sense of superiority and control. Like attracted like, and the circle was vicious. As long as I could focus on fixing them, I could delay fixing myself.

In my search for the answers to what made me tick, I have read the book of every self-help guru and licensed psychologist of the past 20 years! I've bought the tapes and watched the videos! I've read some pretty amazing books, but in all the books I have read through the years, I have never read a statement more true than this one from *Love the Life you Live*, by Les Parrott and Neil Clark Warren.

"...your relationships can only be as healthy as the least healthy person in them."

Now that is truth with a capital T! I had been searching for years for that state of emotional health that I so longed for. Regardless of where I turned to find answers, I found only temporary band-aids that momentarily eased my frustration. So, where do you begin to see yourself as God sees you and to understand your origin of worthiness? Well, as Daddy used to say,... "When in doubt, consult the owner's manual"!

Jesus gave us the foundation for that answer in the first part of that verse... "Love the Lord your God with all your passion and prayer and intelligence." I have learned that only when we first love the Lord with all that we are will our lives start making sense. Hadn't I done that? I had heard this scripture all of my life, but as many that grow up hearing and memorizing scripture, after awhile you can fall into listening with a "yada, yada, yada" sort of attitude. We tend to make our plans, set our goals and then ask God to bless them with His seal of approval. Whether He does or not, we often forge ahead and wonder what happened when things fall apart. What does it mean to love the Lord with all our passion and prayer and intelligence? I have come to learn that until we can let go of all of our plans and dreams and ask God only for what *He* wants for us, we probably aren't loving Him with all that we are. It's a process of maturity when one learns to wait until He opens doors, and then walks through them when He opens them, whether we understand what's going on or not!

Beyond My Yesterdays

When we become passionate and prayerful in learning about God, He will shed light into those dark caverns of our psyche and reveal the areas that need to be dealt with. Like I said before, when you know *Him*, you *know* when He's talking to you! He asks us to learn to love Him with a passion. He asks us to be prayerful about it. And He asks us to be *intelligent* in our love for Him. God doesn't want puppet Christians, where we just hang there and He pulls all the strings! He wants people that have the sense to question and the desire to search for the truth. He gave us minds to use! I can tell you that finding the answers for our lives isn't always easy, but if we're diligent, looking back it's always worth the journey.

Through many years and many different lessons, God showed me that I am not only *worthy* of love, but that I am *perfect*! Not in myself, but through what Christ did for me on the cross. God doesn't look at me and see my failures, any more than He looked at the woman at the well and saw hers. He simply used our failures to illustrate that He sees and knows all! *He* already understands what makes us do what we do. He wasn't concerned about her past. He isn't concerned about mine! What he *is* concerned about is our future! He simply had to bring us to a point of dealing with the ghosts of our pasts in order to bring us into a brighter tomorrow. He had to show me that in order not to repeat the sins and mistakes of my past, I had to learn to draw boundaries in my life, especially where men were concerned.

Proverbs 3:12 says "The one whom the Lord loves He corrects, just as a father corrects the son in whom he delights." God had some serious correcting to do with me!

As I began to search for His will through the scriptures and began to truly study the life of Christ, I realized that Jesus was the all time champion of women that ever lived. Throughout the New Testament accounting of Jesus' life on earth, we consistently see Him ministering to the needs of women that were abused, forced to live a life of prostitution, and caught in adultery. Even Mary Magdalene, one of Jesus' closest friends and followers, had been possessed by seven demons before she met Jesus. We can only imagine what horrors she must have endured in the name of survival.

Jesus was a man that wore His heart on His sleeve, and one of my favorite stories of Jesus' love and overwhelming compassion for women is accounted in John 8:3-11.

The religious scholars and Pharisees led in a woman who had been caught in the act of adultery. They stood her in plain sight of everyone and said, "Teacher, this woman was caught red-handed in the act of adultery. Moses, in the Law, gives orders to stone such persons. What do you say?" They were trying to trap him into saying something incriminating so they could bring charges against him.

Jesus bent down and wrote with his finger in the dirt. They kept at him, badgering him. He straightened up and said, "The sinless one among you, go first; Throw the stone." Bending down again, he wrote some more in the dirt.

Hearing that, they walked away, one after another, beginning with the oldest. I find it especially interesting that the *oldest* left first, and that John made a point of drawing our attention to that. Perhaps the oldest had the most to hide and be forgiven for himself.

The woman was left alone. Jesus stood up and spoke to her. "Woman, where are they? Does no one condemn you?"

"No one, Master."

"Neither do I," said Jesus. "Go on your way. From now on, don't sin."

This story has made many scholars throughout history wonder just what exactly it was that Jesus stooped down and wrote in the dirt. I

Beyond My Yesterdays

have heard as many different opinions of what He wrote, as people giving the opinions. You know what that tells me? I think the reason we don't know what He wrote is because it was for her eyes alone, a personal note of love from God to her in her moment of fear. To me, it is an illustration of how He meets each of us wherever we are, in whatever condition we're in, and He ministers to us as though we were the only person on His mind.

He forgave her and then left her with one restriction, one boundary to protect her. In my mind's eye, I see Him saying, "From now on, don't sin," as He took his finger and drew a line in the sand.

Beyond My Yesterdays

Chapter EIGHT

Beyond My Yesterdays

I Surrender All

*E*very failure, every frustration I had ever experienced in my adult life came to a boiling point as I sat in my bed at my parents' house that morning in 2001. I had tried to live a Christian life with all I had in me. I had now given my heart and my love to three different men that were all more concerned with their own agendas than our marriage. Three times the marriages fell apart, as I was left reeling and wondering what went wrong.

It's a funny thing about being so low that someone could scrape you off the sidewalk. When you're down that far, the only place to go is up. For me though, I was so emotionally destroyed that I didn't have the strength to even try again. I didn't have the fortitude to pull myself up by the bootstraps and once again try to rebuild my life. In my heartbroken state of mind, I finally for the first time in my life came to the absolute end of myself. My heart cried out to God as I looked up and gave up. That morning I stopped trying to live the Christian life, and simply let God know that I was there. If He wanted to live in me and through me, it was going to be Him doing it, not me. In that moment, I came to a place of complete and total surrender of all that I was and all that I wasn't, and told God that from that point on, I wasn't making a move without Him.

It was just a few days later that I awoke and went into the kitchen and told my parents that I was leaving the small town where I had known so much pain, and was moving back to California to begin a new life. I wasn't afraid. I just knew that I was supposed to go.

My last husband had demanded and spent every available dime I had ever saved or invested, and I was unemployed. Picking up and moving made no sense whatsoever in my situation, but I trusted that California was where I was supposed to be. Without a question or moment of hesitation, my parents looked at each other and said that they thought it was a good idea. I trust the Holy Spirit in my parents' lives, so this was a huge affirmation to me. Within a couple of months, God had led me to a Christian businesswoman in San Diego that offered me a job that would allow me to move and start over. Leaving that town behind that was so full of painful memories for me proved to be a powerful catalyst in my learning to think positively about the future.

God began to talk with me about my relationship to men. Through prayer and my time studying His word, I made a commitment to myself and to the Lord. I promised the Lord that for a period of one year, the entire year of 2002, I would not date anyone. For one year, I devoted myself to my own personal growth. What I learned about myself and my God through that year was so precious to me, that I wouldn't trade it for the world.

During that year the Lord had convicted me about several issues that needed to be surrendered to Him. He began laying down boundaries for me that would eventually lead me into emotional healing. I listened to every nudge of the Holy Spirit. I tuned my ear to hear His voice, and when I did, I obeyed. For the first time in my life I stopped trying to bend and rationalize scripture to fit my lifestyle. His word was truth. If He said it, I followed it. End of discussion.

God is so incredibly loving and gentle. If we ask Him, he'll be more than happy to show us the areas that we need to work on, but I learned that He will not force us to change. As with our very salvation, He simply offers new life, and it's our job to accept the gift. The first boundary that He showed me that needed to be drawn in my life was

Beyond My Yesterdays

this deep need I had to be accepted. I had spent a lifetime trying to earn peoples love and respect. Looking back, I realized that every move I had made in my adult life from marriage to my drive to succeed in business had been fueled by my need for the approval of others.

As I began to study and pray about my worthiness as a person, the Holy Spirit began to show me that my validation as a person was a settled issue before I was created to walk this earth. The Bible tells me in Psalm 139 that I am so precious to God, that His thoughts towards me outnumber the grains of sand on this earth. Before I was born, He knew the days that were ordained for me. He set into motion this creation of His called "Jeannie" and entered into a communion with me to grow in our relationship together. He knows the number of hairs on my head. He knows when I get up and when I lie down, and every thought I have in between. In fact, my value to Him was so immeasurable that long before I breathed my first breath, God sent His Son to earth to die for me so that every sin ever committed that would effect my life could be forgiven and forgotten for all eternity, ushering in the opportunity for my everlasting emotional growth. Then to top it off, God sent His Holy Spirit to a new change of address. He came to live within a new temple. He came to live within me.

I began to see that my worth as a person wasn't going to be found in a man. It wasn't going to be found in my bank accounts or by how many businesses I had built and sold. It wasn't going to be found in my children or grandchildren. It wasn't going to be found in my abilities or talents. It was only going to be found in one place, in and through the person of Jesus Christ. He alone is what makes me worthy, because of what He did for me at Calvary. I slowly began to see myself as God sees me. When He turns His eyes towards me, He doesn't see my failures *or* my successes, because standing between God and me is His son, Jesus Christ.

I am covered by His holiness, and when God looks my way, all He sees is Jesus. As I began to see myself as He sees me, I drew my first boundary. I stopped listening to the old tapes that played in my head that told me that I wasn't worthy of love or success. I became extremely aware when I was making decisions for either God's approval or man's. I adopted an attitude that the only two opinions that I really cared about were God's and my own. I saw us as partners in my re-creation, with Him as my psychologist and therapist of choice. I began to make decisions that were best for me and my goal to walk within His will for me. With every little victory, I felt myself growing out of the trap that I had lived in for so long.

Another major line that He showed me needed to be drawn in my life was regarding sex. Having been raised as I was, I went into my first marriage playing by God's rules.

Thirteen years later, believing that all of those rules hadn't gotten me anywhere anyway, I began rationalizing that God's word obviously wasn't pertinent to this day and age, and once I started dating again, lowering my standards seemed emotionally far safer to me than living by God's.

In lowering those standards I learned something incredibly interesting and life changing. Sex messes with your brain! Yes, your brain. Looking back over my life, I realized that I married two men that I never would have married had I not been sleeping with them. Hindsight being 20/20, I realized that in joining with another through the intimacy of sex, there is a mystical bond that happens in that exchange of passion. With each of my husbands, I left a part of me behind that I can never recapture. I became emotionally attached to these men through the act of sex, consequently shading every thought, emotion, and judgment I made.

Marriage was designed to be the union of two souls, and sex was designed by God to create a bond that is shared with no one else outside of those two. In obedience to what I felt God was saying to me, I took a personal oath of celibacy, knowing that it might well be for the rest of my life. I had made so many bad personal choices, and there was very little in me that even cared about ever being married again. I knew that unless God sent me His choice of a marriage partner for me somewhere in my distant future that I would never again marry. I knew all too well from personal experience that a marriage with the wrong person is far worse than having no marriage at all.

Synonymous with the boundaries that needed to be drawn in my life was the need for me to surrender my all to a power much higher than myself. As I started taking responsibility for my past choices, I also took responsibility for my future choices. I knew with all that was in me that anything outside of God's will for me was someplace I didn't want to be. I wasn't going to spend any more time rationalizing my way of doing things. I gave it all up. I surrendered the fear. I surrendered control. I surrendered my anger, my need to ask "why?", my need for others approval, my need to succeed financially, everything. I simply let it go.

The very connotation of the word "surrender" is for many a negative one. For someone like me, a type-A sort of personality, surrender feels more like defeat than a peaceful place of release. Perhaps a better word to describe what I experienced through this process is *acceptance*.

The more I've grown, the more I've realized that the process of maturity really is a process of acceptance. The rules of the universe are what they are, formed and put into motion by the hand of God. It took me many years to accept that God is Sovereign. I could accept it or reject it, but I wasn't going to change it! Once I began to accept His will for my life, drawing boundaries where they needed to be drawn, giving up my need to control and manipulate things to my desired outcome, my life began to change. As the old song said, I lost it all to find everything.

It was during that year following my last divorce that God asked me to give up something that at the time was devastating to me. I had been daily listening for the Holy Spirit to direct and mold me. I could sense when He would send little tests my way, almost as though He was helping me to take baby steps into wholeness. Every time I was presented with a situation where I might have previously made an emotionally unprofitable decision, I was keenly aware of His presence and His nudging for me to make a different decision in line with my new surrendered way of thinking. With every victory, I felt stronger, more alive, and growing in my communion with Him. I was starting to so enjoy my newfound power in Him. I truly felt that I could conquer anything with His help. I was feeling more emotionally healthy than I had in almost thirty years, and it felt so incredibly good.

It was in a breakfast meeting of Christian professional women one Thursday morning that God reached into the depths of my soul and asked for the big piece of the puzzle that was holding me back from the future He wanted for me. I don't remember who the speaker was that morning, I don't remember what we ate or the names of all the ladies sitting at my table. All I remember is that after the speaker finished speaking, we were asked to open individual discussions around each table. I was seated at a table with some pretty impressive Christian professional women. They were attorneys, doctors, and business owners. I was listening more than taking an active part in the discussion when something happened to me that I will never forget. As these women were talking, it was as though God put words in their mouths and one after the other was speaking precisely to me. They had no idea of the impact of what they were saying, but God was speaking directly to

Beyond My Yesterdays

me and in an instant, I knew what He wanted of me. I don't know if you've ever felt a call of God on your life, but when you do, there's no denying it. In that instant, out of nowhere, God spoke very directly to my heart and told me that He wanted me to share my story.

Instantly, I burst into tears. He could have asked me for anything in the world, but not *that*. Was He really asking me to surrender and expose my shame? I had spent nearly thirty years making bad choices, and my shame and failure had become my identity. I had moved to California to have a chance to build new relationships where people accepted me at face value, rather than seeing the shame of my past. These people didn't even know about my failures, they just loved me and accepted me for who I was, and it felt so good. I was trying so hard to make new choices and live beyond my past, and now here He was asking me to walk right back into the shame of my past and expose it for everyone to see. I couldn't take it. I had come so far to rebuild, how could He ask this of me? I didn't understand it, but I had come far enough to know that disobedience was not an option. In the length of about three seconds, I surrendered that too.

The poor ladies sitting at my table that morning didn't know what hit them! One minute, they were having a seemingly uneventful conversation, and the next there I was crying a puddle down at the end of the table! They asked me if I was alright. I wasn't, but I had to let them know what had just happened so that they could understand. I told them that I had just felt a very real call of God on my life.

As they congratulated me, I said "You don't understand; I don't want to do this". Every eye turned to me and I had to explain. As I exposed my pain and my past to those ladies, they surrounded me with such compassion and empathy. They prayed for me and encouraged me not to hesitate to do what God was asking of me. As I left and walked out to my car, I felt like I had just been struck by lightening and

I was in shock, literally dazed. What did God mean by "share your story"? I didn't know exactly what it meant, but I was keenly aware that I needed to live in a state of availability if and when He opened the doors for me to share.

It had been over a year since I had begun to tune my ear to listen for His voice. He had exposed many areas of my life that I needed to surrender and change. Every time He had called my name, I had answered yes, even if it was reluctantly! I was emotionally exhausted and infused all at the same time. I had absolutely no idea what He was doing or where He wanted to take me, but I did know one thing.

I was surrendered. Unequivocally, irrevocably surrendered.

Since that day, I have shared my story with many people, some one-on-one, some in a classroom setting, and even some on television. What I have found remarkable is that not once has anyone thrown my experience back at me in judgment and condemnation. Even though I can often read the shock on people's faces, every time the Lord has opened a door for me to share with another, it has resulted in an experience of healing and hope for all involved.

It was about a month after I felt this call of God on my life that I first had the opportunity to share the truth of where I had been and the consequences of my past choices. I knew that I had to write a letter to someone that I didn't even know, but putting myself on the line to write that letter was an incredibly fearful experience for me. I finished the letter and sent it off, not knowing what the outcome would be.

What I learned is that when we are truly surrendered to *His will* for our lives, He will do "exceeding abundantly above all that we can ask or think"... (Ephesians 3:20).

Beyond My Yesterdays

Chapter NINE

Beyond My Yesterdays

A New Beginning

*I*t was New Years Eve, and it had been one year to the date since I had pledged not to date. As I sat in my office at work after everyone else had gone home to celebrate the New Year, I was suddenly aware that it had been a year of no dating, great personal growth, and communion with God like I hadn't known for a long time. I was feeling stronger, as I had settled into my new job and my new life in California. As I reflected back on the previous year, I couldn't help but feel immensely grateful for the healing that had taken place in me during that year. I felt good, I felt peaceful, and I felt a new sense of hope for the future.

Not having a date for New Year's Eve, I wasn't in the same hurry that everyone else had been in to get home. I decided to check my email before going home and before I knew it, I was surfing the web looking at different clothing websites. I believe I was on the Spiegel site when a window popped up on my screen for eHarmony.com. The ad invited me to "fall in love for all the right reasons". As I went to click it off, something caught my eye about the founder of the company, and I began to read. As I read further, I became more and more intrigued with their psychologically based program, and before I knew it, I had signed up for a free personality profile and one month of membership! After not dating for a year, and considering my disastrous choices in the past, I thought it might be fun to see who a computer might match me to! After all, it was safe, I was completely protected. They had no way of finding me, as I was just "Jeannie in San Diego". It seemed like fun, and since I had learned to be honest with myself, I placed an order for my perfect man, hit the submit button, and thought, "That'll never happen"! I was so picky in describing my knight in shining armor, that I was quite certain he didn't exist. My perfect man had to be first and foremost, a man after God's own heart. I would never settle for anything less again. I had already pledged to God that unless He chose a man for me, I wasn't interested in ever marrying again.

I had only signed up for one month and had every intention of letting the membership lapse on Jan.30. During that month I had a couple of matches, but nothing that interested me enough to pursue them. I simply bleeped the prospective matches off my screen and went on with life. Suddenly on Jan. 27th, just a couple of days before I would let my membership lapse, I was matched with "Chuck from Laguna Niguel".

After a few email exchanges through the eHarmony system, I was becoming quite intrigued with this man named Chuck from Laguna Niguel. We appeared to have so much in common, that I knew if we ever met, we'd be the best of friends. It felt wonderful to think that someone that I appeared to be so equally matched with might be out there! Having fun corresponding was adding light to my otherwise mundane daily existence and I really wanted to meet him, but I couldn't do it without first letting him know who I was. I couldn't bear another heartbreak, so it was time to put my cards out on the table. As much as I didn't want to tell him of my past, it was mine to own and I didn't want to hurt him in any way either. So my letter began.

Dear Chuck,

I am writing this in Word format so that I don't lose it over email! I thought that in getting to know each other, you would want to know some of

Beyond My Yesterdays

my personal history, and it would be hard fitting 44 years into the confines of an eharmony email!

You have invited me to ask you anything I would like to know and I appreciate that. Of course eventually, I'd like to know everything about you. I have the feeling that if we got together, we could probably talk for days on end about many different subjects and just begin to get a glimpse into each other's personalities and experiences!

As I told you before, I was born in...

I spilled it all. I told him about my entire life from my birth to the present day, including my heartbreak over each marriage. Even though Chuck was still a stranger to me, sharing my story with him was an extremely painful and embarrassing thing to do. The letter continued...

A year ago, I still felt that all the king's horses and all the king's men could never put me back together again. But this has been a year of healing and divinely inspired insight into why I made the choices in my past that I did. I've turned down every invitation to date since my last divorce. It's been my time for reflection and prayer. Now I see that the choices I made, looking for significance through man's approval, were never what I needed. God loves me and I love me and that's where I needed to be all along. My purpose in life is different now. My future will be different. My life is now on the altar, open to whatever the Lord has for me.

Will I ever marry again? I don't know. That's up to Him. Am I looking? Not really. Am I closed to it? No. Am I ready for some fun and friendship? Absolutely!

I would love to continue our correspondence and build a friendship, Chuck. However, if you'd rather not pursue it, I understand. I have absolutely no idea

of your past and the hurts you've known, but I want you to know that I am
praying for you. I sense a spirit of kindness and God's love in you and wish
you the very best.

I hope you'll pray for me too.

Keep smiling!

Jeannie

I waited. This was the first time I had laid my life bare for anyone, and I completely expected him to return a nice "Thanks, but no
thanks" email, and then promptly bleep me off his screen. Instead, I
received his reply the next day....

Hi Jeannie,

I feel so honored and humble to have been given the privilege of your sharing
so candidly with me your personal history. My heart grieved for you but praised
God for what He has done to restore you. I have a story of my own with its
share of heartaches and misguided judgments. Like you, for the treasures of my
two kids and now, grandchildren, it's water under the bridge. Like our salva-
tion, Romans 8:18 "I consider that our present sufferings are not worth com-
paring with the glory that will be revealed in us". I want you to know that I
felt only more endeared to you within the details of what you shared with me.

His letter went on, but it was that first paragraph that reduced me
to tears. His reply to me was such a gift, as though God was telling me
that in following Him there was hope for my future. I don't think it
was coincidence that Chuck was the first person that I shared my story
with. I knew I had to meet him.

Beyond My Yesterdays

It was a beautiful Sunday afternoon in Southern California when I walked into the lobby of the Hotel Del Coronado in San Diego. We had arranged to meet there, have lunch and get to know each other a bit better. As I walked into the lobby, it was bustling with families and vacationers enjoying a warm sunny afternoon. The place was buzzing, but all I could think about was finding "Chuck from Laguna Niguel"! I had only seen a picture of him, so wasn't sure if I'd recognize him when I saw him. As my eyes scanned the room, suddenly my gaze stopped on the silhouette of a man on the far side of the lobby. I couldn't see his face, as he was backlit by the sunlight streaming into the room from behind him, but somehow I knew it was him. As I crossed the lobby, he saw me and came out to meet me. The first time we met, we embraced as though we were old friends. That lunch at the Del that day turned into seven hours of talking, laughing, and sharing our stories with each other.

As Chuck and I began to build our friendship, I was so taken with his strong, yet gentle spirit. My father was the only other man that had ever treated me with the kind of respect and dignity that Chuck did. I knew this relationship was different, but I still knew that I had a reputation of choosing partners that I didn't belong with, so I made a choice to involve the people that loved me most in my decision to start dating Chuck. I opened all of the correspondence between us to my parents, my sister, and my daughter. If any of them saw a red flag anywhere, I wanted to know before my heart got involved any further. I asked to meet Chuck's family on our second date, and made arrangements for him to meet mine shortly after. With every turn, my heart was becoming more peaceful, as my family fell in love with him. God was affirming this relationship to me from every possible angle, and we all knew it was sent from Him.

On June 28, 2003, Chuck and I exchanged wedding vows with only our families present. As they stood in a circle surrounding us, we promised to love and live only for God and each other until "death do us part". The day I married Chuck was the happiest day of my life. Although we had both recited vows with others before, only to watch our dreams go up in smoke, this time was different. We both knew in our hearts that this time, it wasn't something that we had manipulated to make happen. We had both come to a point before meeting each other of total and complete surrender to God for our individual lives, and we both knew He alone had led us to that moment of becoming man and wife.

In my life, I have known such bitter sorrow, that I would never wish my past experiences on anyone. I also have known joy beyond what I could have ever dreamed. Now as I fall asleep each night in the arms of a man that truly loves me and is as committed to our marriage as I am, I can't help but feel a soulful gratitude for what God has brought me through and taught me in the process. Chuck says that God knew that my story wouldn't be complete without a happy ending!

The night that Chuck asked me to marry him, he went to painstaking detail to recreate that first moment that we met in the lobby of the Hotel Del. He was waiting for me exactly where he had been waiting that first Sunday afternoon. We walked the same walks, ate in the same restaurant, walked out to the same bench by the water to watch the sunset. This time though as we sat by the water, Chuck asked me to be his wife, and slipped a diamond onto my finger. In that moment, all my fears of ever making another mistake in choosing a marriage partner melted away forever. I knew beyond the shadow of a doubt that God had brought me to the end of this particular "desert" period in my life, as He had opened for me an oasis of love and sanctuary in Chuck.

Before we married, I gave Chuck a full scale reproduction of King Arthur's Excalibur sword with a plaque that hangs beside it. On the plaque I penned these words...

Beyond My Yesterdays

Once upon a time in a land far away, lived a boy that would be king. In the town square of the village was a sword embedded in a stone and as legend tells, only the true ruler of the land would possess the power to remove the sword from the stone. Although many tried valiantly to draw the sword from the grip of the stone, only Arthur succeeded in the quest, as he was destined to rule the land as a king of noble character and uncommon valor. Thus, the legend of King Arthur of Camelot was born.

Once upon a heart many years hence, lived a maiden whose heart had grown as cold and hard as stone, having been pierced so deeply that she thought it could never again live free of the anguish of the past. Though some tried to remove the sword from her heart, she knew that only her Lord would have the power to send the one that could soften her heart with his love, healing the piercing pain of years gone by.

Her Lord brought that man to her. Where only God could fill the void in her heart, the man of her heart dried her tears and gave her a reason to rejoice again. His strength of character and loving devotion first to God, and then to her gave her cause to believe again in the healing empowerment of love. In her eyes, he was not a mere man, but a king...a man among men that would forever hold the key to the kingdom of her heart.

She gifted him a sword, like that of King Arthur's to hang forever in the room of their marriage bed as a reminder of all that he was to her...the leader of their home, her knight in shining armor, the hero of her heart.

And they lived happily ever after.........

Beyond My Yesterdays

EPILOGUE

This is a tale of two women separated by two thousand years of history, but intrinsically woven together by one shared experience. Jesus met both of them at their point of deepest need and they were never the same again.

T

he Bible doesn't tell us much of what happened to the Samaritan women after she ran from the well that day. The rest of her story is one we will never know in this lifetime. One thing I do know however is that her story is the story of *many of us.* The circumstances may be different, but deep in the hearts of most of us lie regrets over past choices and things we wish we would have done differently. Many of us have been the victims of someone else's selfish and disturbed behaviors. Many of us still live with the daily consequences of broken relationships and dreams, even years after the events that once threatened to destroy us.

The good news is that the same Jesus that met the Samaritan woman that day at the well is still in the business of mending lives and molding souls into experiencing God's very best for them. *With God, it's never too late!*

If sharing my story encourages *one* soul in their journey to look heavenward and trust in the almighty sovereignty of a God that knows everything about you and loves you just as you are, then all is as it should be. Wherever you may be on your journey, know that there is a God who loves you more than you could possibly imagine that wants to take you under His protective wing and guide you into a brighter future.

He is as close as your heart; you simply need to open it to Him. You may have some serious soul searching to do and changes to make before your life becomes what you want it to be, but I can guarantee you that years from now when you look back on the process, you will be grateful for the experience of having walked your path with your hand in His. Blessings on your journey!

Beyond My Yesterdays

*D*ear Friend,

If you are reading these words, I want you to know how my heart longs to encourage you on your journey. In this moment, if we could just sit down and have a cup of tea together, I would want you to know this.

It occurs to me that one that has endured the gut-wrenching devastation of watching their life fall apart for any number of reasons might read a story like mine and think, "Well Jeannie, good for you. Your story turned out alright, but you don't know what I've endured or what I still have to deal with in my future". You're right. No one can ever truly know what it means to endure someone else's agony.

You are the only one that can walk your journey, but I want to encourage you in doing just that. You see, I know that when you are in the mental and emotional throws of just getting through one day at a time, hoping you can just hang on, that it is very hard to see the light at the end of the tunnel. It can be very hard to believe that it will turn out alright for you. I know. I was in that tunnel for a very long time. I lost all hope of ever seeing my dreams become reality. If I had known even one person that had walked that path before me and could have said to me what I'm saying to you right now, it would have helped. So, this is what I want you to know.

- *You are beautiful.* You are worthy of every wonderful thing that life has to offer simply because you *are*. You see, the God that formed you in your mother's womb, that knit every piece of sinew, bone, and muscle together, started blood flowing through each organ in your body and then breathed life into you, knew *exactly* what He was doing. Just as He did during the creation of the world, He looked at you upon your creation and saw that you were *very* good. He chose your hair color, the color of your skin, your unique talents and abilities, and the place of your birth. He knew you would have some tough obstacles to overcome in life, but He also knew that you would have the inner strength to get beyond them and become a victor over anything and *anyone* that ever tried to keep you down. That fighting spirit in you is the spirit of the living God. Believe in yourself.

- *You are not alone.* I know that it can feel that way, but the very fact that you're reading these words right now proves otherwise. You see, the very God that called me to share my story, knew that you would be reading this right now. He's been thinking of you for a very long time, and wants to walk your journey with you. All you need to do is open your mind to the possibility of getting to know Him. I would suggest that you get a copy of "The Message" by Eugene H. Peterson - a translation of the Bible written in everyday language - and start reading in the middle of the book. Try Matthew, Mark, Luke and John. Learn about Him. Pray. Throw out all your pre-conceived ideas about church and simply ask Him to reveal *Himself* to you. Don't be surprised when people start coming into your life to help you on your journey!

* *You will get beyond your yesterdays!* The beauty of God is that He's the same yesterday, today and forever. That means that when He promises He'll guide us into a new tomorrow, that promise is for *everyone* that seeks Him and earnestly wants a relationship with Him. That means you! Just as the sun comes up every morning and goes down at dusk, He is always the same. Just as He's done it for me and millions of others, He will do it for you!

* *You have a purpose to fulfill!* I predict that there will come a day in your life where, like me, you will look back and see that there was a reason for everything that happened in your life. There may be a dream inside of you that only you know about. Something on a level so deep that you may not even realize it; something that you just *feel* you were born to do. I believe that God created you exactly as you are to accomplish the unique purpose that is yours to contribute on this earth. Every wonderful attribute of your personality, as well as every trial you've ever overcome are going to come together at some point to make you uniquely qualified for the mark you will make on this world. Believe in His guidance, believe in His timing, and believe in yourself! He has a plan for you!

* *Reclaim the spirit that is you!* Learn to love yourself. I remember when I discovered this for myself. I had always

loved and nurtured everyone around me, but for so long it had been unacceptable in my situation to nurture my own dreams, my own spirit. One day as I was pining away over the loss of a man in my life and just wanting so badly for someone to send me flowers, I had an epiphany. I called the florist and sent myself a beautiful bouquet of spring flowers that sat on my desk for a week and reminded me that I was responsible for my own happiness and well-being. With every breath of that wonderful floral scent that drifted into my lungs, I felt I was breathing new life into my spirit. Over time, I learned to treat myself as well as I would treat others. This may seem silly, but giving yourself permission to take care of yourself can have a profound impact on your ability to start the healing process. You need to take care of yourself; mind, spirit and body.

- **Relax.** I have a girlfriend that said her father's favorite scripture is "and it came to pass...."! *Everything* eventually passes. Everything except the love. The Bible tells us that heaven and earth will eventually pass away, but that love never will. If you can learn to focus on God's love in you and the love that's around you, and realize that when it's all said and done, nothing else really matters, then you've found the secret to life. Whatever situation you're in today, there is a promise of tomorrow. Never give up believing that. Someone may have robbed you of your past, but you hold the key to your future, and it can still become what you want it to be!

Beyond My Yesterdays

I don't want you to feel like you're out there without a lifeline. There are many great churches and support groups filled with people just like us. I would encourage you to find a good one and plug into it. There are also many, many great books on the market that can help you in your process. Some of my favorites are by T.D. Jakes. For women, be sure to read "Woman Thou Art Loosed" and "The Lady, Her Lover, and Her Lord". Others that are fabulous are Dr. Phil McGraw's "Self Matters" and "Relationship Rescue". Take time to read. Filling your mind with helpful insight and instruction will do far more for your healing than replaying over and over in your mind the events that have caused you such pain. Remember, this is a new day. If you learn new habits that bring positive reinforcement into your daily life, I can guarantee that you will grow far beyond the pain of today.

I have also created a blog, just to keep in touch and encourage you on your journey. I hope you will sign up to receive it automatically, so that you are always reminded that there is someone out there that loves you and cares about your progress.

Perhaps one day we will meet. If not on this side of heaven, then I hope we'll meet there. I look forward to the day that I will look into your eyes, take your hand in mine, and without one word exchanged between us, know that in spite of everything and everyone that may have tried to keep us down, we overcame....*together*.

God bless you,

Beyond My Yesterdays

GAIN STRENGTH
IN A CONTINUOUS
CIRCLE OF FRIENDS!

*W*ant to be part of Jeannie's circle of friends? Every month, Jeannie shares through her blog, new anecdotes and insights into experiencing life together! As part of Jeannie's inner circle, you'll receive genuine support for your journey, as Jeannie shares insights from her own experiences and daily walk with God.

- Be encouraged by Jeannie's heartfelt thoughts of inspiration...
- Learn how to bring Jeannie to speak at your next event...
- Post your thoughts on Jeannie's site...
- Be the first to know about new book introductions and upcoming special events!

Sign up today, and don't miss a thing!

www.JeannieKeneley.com